P9-DCR-320

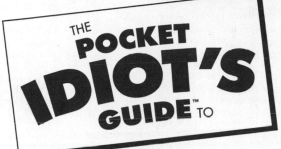

THE POCKET IDIOT'S GUIDE TO

Italian
Phrases

Second Edition

by Gabrielle Ann Euvino

ALPHA

A member of Penguin Group (USA) Inc.

ALPHA BOOKS

Published by the Penguin Group

Penguin Group (USA) Inc., 375 Hudson Street, New York, New York 10014, U.S.A.

Penguin Group (Canada), 10 Alcorn Avenue, Toronto, Ontario, Canada M4V 3B2 (a division of Pearson Penguin Canada Inc.)

Penguin Books Ltd, 80 Strand, London WC2R 0RL, England

Penguin Ireland, 25 St Stephen's Green, Dublin 2, Ireland (a division of Penguin Books Ltd)

Penguin Group (Australia), 250 Camberwell Road, Camberwell, Victoria 3124, Australia (a division of Pearson Australia Group Pty Ltd)

Penguin Books India Pvt Ltd, 11 Community Centre, Panchsheel Park, New Delhi—110 017, India

Penguin Group (NZ), cnr Airborne and Rosedale Roads, Albany, Auckland 1310, New Zealand (a division of Pearson New Zealand Ltd)

Penguin Books (South Africa) (Pty) Ltd, 24 Sturdee Avenue, Rosebank, Johannesburg 2196, South Africa

Penguin Books Ltd, Registered Offices: 80 Strand, London WC2R 0RL, England

Copyright © 2005 by Gabrielle Ann Euvino

THE POCKET IDIOT'S GUIDE TO and Design are trademarks of Penguin Group (USA) Inc.

International Standard Book Number: 1-59257-379-7
Library of Congress Catalog Card Number: 2005925279

08 07 06   8 7 6 5 4

Interpretation of the printing code: The rightmost number of the first series of numbers is the year of the book's printing; the rightmost number of the second series of numbers is the number of the book's printing. For example, a printing code of 05-1 shows that the first printing occurred in 2005.

Printed in the United States of America

Note: This publication contains the opinions and ideas of its author. It is intended to provide helpful and informative material on the subject matter covered. It is sold with the understanding that the author and publisher are not engaged in rendering professional services in the book. If the reader requires personal assistance or advice, a competent professional should be consulted.

The author and publisher specifically disclaim any responsibility for any liability, loss, or risk, personal or otherwise, which is incurred as a consequence, directly or indirectly, of the use and application of any of the contents of this book.

To my great Aunt Clara Kaye.

*A special welcome to Sabine Anya, my angel,
born March 8, 2005.*

Contents

Introduction

Learning Italian is no more difficult than rolling out your own pasta dough and making hand-made tortellini. After you know how to do it, it's easy and a lot of fun. Let me remind you that you learned how to speak English long before you were taught how to identify parts of speech. If you allow the intuitive process to guide you, you will be speaking Italian in no time.

Here are a few suggestions to enhance your language study:

- Invest in a good bilingual dictionary, preferably one printed in Italy, such as the Garzanti or Zanichelli Italian/English dictionaries. Langenscheidt also produces an excellent pocket Italian/English dictionary.

- Call your local university and investigate whether it has an Italian department. Find out whether it has a mailing list for events, and make a point of meeting other "Italophiles."

- Rent an Italian movie every week. Listen to the actors and read the subtitles while you try to decipher the Italian words within each sentence. Isolate words that are repeated.

- Pick up a box of Italian language flash cards at any bookstore, or make your own using that unused box of business cards from your old job.

- Listen to the Italian news station, RAI, while you clean your house. If you must spend a lot of time in the car, invest in language tapes and put that commute to good use.

- Sign up for an online Italian language newsletter such as the About Italian Language site: http://italian.about.com.

About This Book

This book lists helpful vocabulary and phrases and tells you exactly what you need to say (and how to say it) in myriad situations: at the train station, at your hotel, in a restaurant, at the pharmacy, and so on. It also summarizes grammar, vocabulary, and verbs in the most concise manner possible, explaining how it all works and what you can do to start speaking the language immediately. I've also improved the pronunciation guide by adding bold to the stressed syllables.

Extras to Help You Along

Besides the idiomatic expressions, helpful phrases, lists of vocabulary words, and grammar tips, this book provides useful information in sidebars throughout the text. These elements are distinguished by the following icons:

La Bella Lingua

Specialized terminology and interesting anecdotes about the Italian language.

What's What

Useful grammatical terms and suggestions on how to modify phrases.

Attenzione!

Highlights potential grammatical faux pas and other linguistic challenges.

When in Roma ...

Specifics related to customs, traditions, and other useful travel information.

Acknowledgments

Special thanks to Oriana Moltisanti and her sister Katia Moltisanti Tennyson for their meticulous technical edits, Stefano Spadoni for his continued support, and GianPaolo Roseghini for his contribution. In addition, the author gratefully acknowledges the Alpha team that made this book happen: Paul Dinas, Megan Douglass, Jennifer Moore, and Keith Cline ... *mille grazie!* And of course, I could never have managed without the unconditional love of my canine companions Dante the Great Dane and Virgilio the Pug.

Trademarks

Say It Like You See It

In This Chapter

- An Italian pronunciation guide
- The Italian alphabet
- Important Italian cognates
- Basic grammar

Say it like you see it—that's the general rule. This chapter shows you the in's and out's of Italian pronunciation. You'll see that Italian is not only fun, but also easy to learn, especially when you understand the basic ground rules.

I've also included an overview of Italian grammar that shows you how to manipulate the *frasi* ("phrases"; pronounced frah-zee) and vocabulary included in this book to suit your needs.

Pronouncing Italian Words

In Italian, the written language you read with your eyes and the spoken language you pronounce with your mouth are practically one and the same; what you see is what you say.

The key is in keeping in mind the basic differences between the English and Italian rules of pronunciation. For example, in Italian, the word *cinema* is written exactly the same as in English; however, in Italian it is pronounced **chee**-neh-mah. The same *ci* is used in the popular greeting *ciao*. Conversely, *ch* in Italian is pronounced as a *k*, as in the word *Chianti*.

La Bella Lingua

If you're unsure of how to pronounce something, remember what you *do* know; ci like *ciao*, ch like *Chianti*. Wherever you see a particular letter combination that has you wondering, go back to a word with which you're already familiar.

The fun part is in the roll of your R's, but please don't overdue it! Keep in mind that double consonants (*anno*, *birra*, *panna*) should be emphasized and held, but always pronounced as one sound.

Getting the Accent

Italian uses the grave accent (`), pronounced grav, on words where the stress falls on the final syllable: *caffè*, *città*, *università*.

You may also see the acute accent (´) used (especially in older text and phrasebooks), particularly with the words *benché* (although) and *perché* (because/why).

The written accent is also used to distinguish several Italian words from others that have the same spelling but a different meaning. These basic examples are all useful vocabulary words to include in your Italian lexicon.

è	is	e	and
sì	yes	si	oneself
dà	gives	da	from
sè	himself	se	if
là	there	la	the
lì	there	li	the
né	nor	ne	some

The following examples illustrate how an apostrophe is often used to indicate the dropping of a final vowel. When listening to Italian speakers, remember that nouns are often preceded by an article such as *l'* or *la*, both of which signify "the" and which will affect how you hear a particular word.

l'animale instead of *lo animale* (the animal)

d'Italia instead of *di Italia* (of Italy)

dov'è instead of *dove è* (where is)

> ### What's What
>
> Some Italian letter combinations are seldom found in English. These sounds include the *gl* combination in words such as *figlio* (son; pronounced fee-lyoh); the word *gli* (the; pronounced ylee, like the *ll* in the English word *million*); and the *gn* combination, seen in words such as *gnocchi* (potato dumplings; pronounced nyoh-kee) and *bagno* (bathroom; pronounced bah-nyoh, like the *ny* sound in *canyon* or the *ni* sound in *onion*).

Stress

Wherever there is no accent telling you where the emphasis should go, you'll have to know which syllable should be stressed. In general, keep these rules in mind:

- Most Italian words are emphasized on the *next-to-last* syllable. Examples include *studente* (stoo-**den**-teh) and *viaggio* (vee-**ah**-joh).

- Each syllable in words such as *casa* (kah-zah) are generally given equal emphasis. Examples include *pizza* (pee-tsah) and *futball* (foot-ball).

- Some words are accented on the third-, fourth-, or fifth-to-last syllable. Your Italian-English dictionary should indicate these irregularities, usually with an accent placed over the stressed syllable or a dot placed below it.

Italian ABCs

The Italian language uses the Latin alphabet. Unlike English, however, the Italian alphabet contains only 21 letters, borrowing the letters *j*, *k*, *w*, *x*, and *y* for words of foreign origin.

A Is for *Ancona*

When spelling out words, Italians use the names of Italian cities whenever *possibile*. For example, *A come Ancona, I come Imola, T come Torino* … (*A* as in *Ancona*, *I* as in *Imola*, *T* as in *Torino* …), and so on.

La Bella Lingua

A practical way of remembering the *alfabeto* is to learn how to spell your name in Italian, particularly useful when making *prenotazioni* (reservations) on the *telefono*.

The Italian equivalent is given beside the English letter. The stressed syllable is in **bold.** Examples of foreign letters are given with commonly used nouns.

Letter	Italian Name	Pronunciation of Letter	Example	Pronunciation
A	a	ah	Ancona	ahn-**koh**-nah
B	bi	bee	Bologna	boh-**loh**-nyah
C	ci	chee	Cagliari	**kahl**-yah-ree
D	di	dee	Domo-dossola	doh-moh-**doh**-soh-lah
E	e	eh	Empoli	**em**-poh-lee
F	effe	ehf-feh	Firenze	fee-**ren**-zeh
G	gi	jee	Genova	**jeh**-noh-vah
H	acca	ahk-kah	hotel	oh-tel
I	i	ee	Imola	**ee**-moh-lah
J*	i lunga	ee loon-gah	jolly	jah-lee
K*	cappa	kap-pah	kaiser	ky-zer
L	elle	ehl-leh	Livorno	lee-**vor**-noh
M	emme	ehm-meh	Milano	mee-**lah**-noh
N	enne	ehn-neh	Napoli	**nah**-poh-lee
O	o	oh	Otranto	oh-**tran**-toh
P	pi	pee	Palermo	pah-**ler**-moh
Q	cu	koo	quaderno	kwah-**der**-noh
R	erre	ehr-reh	Roma	roh-mah
S	esse	ehs-seh	Sassari	**sah**-sah-ree
T	ti	tee	Torino	toh-**ree**-noh
U	u	oo	Udine	**oo**-dee-neh
V	vu	voo	Venezia	veh-**neh**-zee-ah
W*	doppia vu	**dohp**-pee-yah voo	Washington	**wash**-eeng-ton
X*	ics	eeks	raggi-x	raj-jee eek-say

Letter	Italian Name	Pronunciation of Letter	Example	Pronunciation
Y*	ipsilon	**eep**-see-lohn	York	york
Z	zeta	zeh-tah	Zaraebra	zah-**ray**-brah

*These letters have been borrowed from other languages.

Vocalize Your *Vocali:* Vowels

Italian vowels should be pronounced clearly and tend to be open. Although variations exist, for your purposes the following table should do the trick.

Italian Vowel	Sound	Example	Pronunciation
a	ah	artista	ar-**tee**-stah
e	eh	elefante	eh-leh-**fahn**-teh
i	ee	isola	**ee**-zoh-lah
o	oh	opera	**oh**-peh-rah
u	oo	uno	oo-noh

Italian Consonants

The following examples demonstrate most of the different letter *combinazioni* that you'll encounter. Assume that any letters not included follow the English pattern of pronunciation. For example, the letter *b* will always be pronounced the same, regardless the letters that follow.

Letter	Sound	Example	Pronunciation	English
c + a, o, u	hard c (as in *cat*)	candela	kahn-**deh**-lah	candle
c + e, i	ch (as in chest)	centro	chen-troh	center/downtown
ch	hard c (as in cat)	Chianti	kee-**ahn**-tee	Chianti
g + a, o, u	hard g (as in go)	Gabriella	gah-bree-**ehl**-lah	Gabriella
g + e, i	jay (as in jet)	Giorgio	jor-joh	Giorgio
gli	ylee (as in million)	figlio	fee-lyoh	son
gn	nyah (as in onion)	gnocchi	nyoh-kee	potato dumplings
h (called acca)	silent	hotel	oh-tel	hotel
s (at the beginning of a word)	ess (as in see)	serpente	ser-**pen**-teh	snake
s	zee (as in busy)	casa	kah-zah	home
sc + a, o	sk	scala	skah-lah	stair
sc + e, i	sh	scena	sheh-nah	scene

Grammar 101

Understanding a few basic facts about *la grammatica* will help you make better sense of what you will hear when you travel through Italy. After you understand the essentials, you'll be able to form Italian *frasi* with relative ease.

Nouns

In Italian, the word *nome* means "name" as well as "noun." In Italian, every *nome* (noun) is designated as masculine or feminine and is either singular or plural. Usually you can tell both a noun's *gender* and its *number* by looking at the ending. Some nouns can be either masculine or feminine, such as the words *artista* (artist), *parente* (relative), and *turista* (tourist).

Gender

The gender of a noun affects its relationship with other words in a sentence, including adjectives. Similar to other Romance languages, nouns and adjectives must always agree in number and gender. If the noun is masculine, it usually ends in *-o*; if a noun is feminine, it usually ends in *-a*. The adjective follows suit. For example, *il gatto nero* literally translates to "the cat black." Likewise, with feminine nouns, the adjective reflects the gender, as in *la casa bianca* ("the house white"). (Similar to Spanish and French, most—not all—Italian nouns are followed by the adjective.)

Some singular nouns and adjectives end in *-e*, such as *l'animale* (m.) ("the animal") and *la stazione* (f.) ("the station"). You can generally infer the gender by studying the noun markers, although sometimes straight memorization is best.

More Is More: Making Plurals

In Italian, the ending must always reflect the number and gender of the noun. The following table illustrates how regular endings change in the plural. Again, keep in mind that if a noun ends in -*o*, it is generally masculine; if a noun ends in -*a*, it is generally feminine. Nouns ending in -*e* can be either gender.

Singular Ending		Plural Ending	Singular Noun		Plural Noun
-o	→	-i	ragazz*o*	→	ragazz*i*
-a	→	-e	donn*a*	→	donn*e*
-ca	→	-che	am*ica*	→	ami*che*
-e	→	-i	can*e*	→	can*i*

Noun Markers

Just about every Italian noun is preceded by a noun marker. These noun markers provide clues as to whether a noun is *masculine* (m.) or *feminine* (f.), *singular* (s.) or *plural* (p.). Both the indefinite and definite articles are examples of noun markers.

An Indefinite Article (A, An)

The following indefinite articles express *a*, *an*, or *one*. Remember that an indefinite article is only used before *singular* nouns. Here are some rules to live by:

Masculine:

Un is used before all singular masculine nouns beginning with either a consonant or a vowel, such as *un palazzo* (a building), *un signore* (a gentleman), and *un animale* (animal), except those nouns beginning with a *z* or an *s* followed by a consonant.

Uno follows the same rules as the definite article *lo* (discussed in the next section) and is used before singular masculine nouns beginning with a *z* or an *s* followed by a consonant, such as *uno zio* (an uncle) and *uno stadio* (a stadium).

Feminine:

Una is used before any feminine noun beginning with a consonant, such as *una farfalla* (a butterfly), *una storia* (a story), and *una strada* (a street).

Un' is the equivalent of *an* in English and is used before all feminine nouns beginning with a vowel, such as *un'italiana* (an Italian woman), *un'amica* (a friend), and *un'opera* (an opera).

The Definite Articles

Italian definite articles follow very specific rules. Follow the examples in the following table. (Or not. Whatever makes you happy.)

Singular Definite Articles	Plural Definite Articles
Il is used in front of most singular, masculine nouns that begin with a consonant.*	**I** is used in front of most plural, masculine nouns that begin with a consonant.*
il ragazzo (the boy)	i ragazzi (the boys)
il sole (the sun)	i libri (the books)
il vino (the wine)	i gatti (the cats)
Lo is used in front of all singular, masculine nouns that begin with a *z* or an *s* followed by a consonant.	**Gli** (pronounced ylee as in *million*) is used in front of all masculine plural nouns that use either **lo** or **l'** in the singular.
lo zio (the uncle)	gli zii (the uncles)
lo studente (the student)	gli studenti (the students)
	gli alberi (the trees)
	gli animali (the animals)
L' is used in front of all singular nouns—whether masculine or feminine— that begin with a vowel.	
l'albero m. (the tree)	
l'animale m. (the animal)	
l'opera f. (the opera; the work)	
La is used in front of all other singular, feminine nouns.	**Le** is used in front of *all* plural, feminine nouns.
la ragazza (the girl)	le ragazze (the girls)
la macchina (the car)	le macchine (the cars)
	le opere (the operas; the works)

*Except z or an s followed by a consonant

Che Bello! Adjectives

Italian adjectives follow the same general rules as nouns, and they must agree in gender and number with the nouns they describe. Similar to Italian nouns, some singular adjectives end in *-e*.

Singular Ending		Plural Ending	Singular Adjective		Plural Adjective
-o	→	-i	famos*o*	→	famos*i*
-a	→	-e	curios*a*	→	curios*e*
-ca	→	-che	magnifi*ca*	→	magnifi*che*
-e	→	-i	intelligent*e*	→	intelligent*i*

When in Roma ...

Che bello! is one of those *espressioni* you can use just about anywhere you go in Italy. It literally means "what beauty!" If the object of your praise is feminine, you would say *Che bella!*

Connect It All with Prepositions

Prepositions show the relationship between a noun and another word in a sentence. Prepositions are highly idiomatic (meaning they follow their own set of rules) and should be remembered within a context, rather than exclusively memorized.

The most important prepositions are as follows.

Italian Preposition	English Preposition	Example
a	to/at/in	Andiamo a Roma. (We're going to Rome.)
con	with	Vado con Roberto. (I am going with Roberto.)
da	from/by	Leonardo da Vinci (Leonardo from Vinci)
di	of/from	Sono di New York. (I am from New York.)
in	in/to/by	Viaggiamo in Italia. (We are traveling to Italy.)
per	for	Questo regalo è per te. (This present is for you.)
su	on	Il libro sta sulla* scrivania. (The book is on the desk.)

su + la = sulla (a contraction)

Mamma Mia! Possession

In Italian, a possessive adjective must always be followed by a noun, which is generally preceded by an article. For example, *la mia casa* literally translates to "the my house." Both the possessor and what is possessed must agree in *gender* and *number*.

| Possessive | Singular | | Plural | |
Adjective	Masculine	Feminine	Masculine	Feminine
my	il mio	la mia	i miei	le mie
your	il tuo	la tua	i tuoi	le tue
his/her/its	il suo	la sua	i suoi	le sue
Your (polite)*	il Suo	la Sua	i Suoi	le Sue
our	il nostro	la nostra	i nostri	le nostre
your	il vostro	la vostra	i vostri	le vostre
their	il loro	la loro	i loro	le loro

Notice that the third person singular possessive adjectives la sua *and* il suo *can mean both his and her.*

Attenzione!

When using possessives to talk about your *famiglia*, there's no need to use an article, such as when you say *Mamma mia!*

Italian Subject Pronouns

Italian subject pronouns are often omitted because the endings indicate the subject. For example, *Viaggiamo in Italia* literally translates to "We are traveling to Italy." The *-iamo* ending from the verb tells us that the subject is *noi* (we).

Italian	English
io	I
tu	you, informal
lui/lei/Lei*	he/she/you (polite)
noi	we
voi	you (plural)
loro	they

*The pronoun Lei (with a capital L) signifies "you" (polite, or formal); the pronoun lei signifies "she."

You and You and You

There are actually four forms of *you* in Italian. If you're speaking with a friend, you use *tu*. If you're speaking to a professor or authority figure, you use *Lei*. Note the following rules regarding *you:*

- *Tu* is used in informal settings with friends and relatives or when adults address children.

- *Lei* is the polite form of you, and is used with strangers and persons in authority and to show respect or maintain a more formal relationship with someone. It is always capitalized to distinguish it from the pronoun *lei*, meaning "she."

- *Voi* is primarily used to address a group of people, although it can still be used as a formal way of addressing an individual, especially in the south.

● *Loro* is used in rare cases when an extreme form of politeness is required, either when addressing a group of people or someone in a high position, such as a president or the pope. It was once used more commonly and can still be heard in old films.

What's What

Remember this: If you're talking about yourself, your verb will always end in *-o*, such as when you say to someone *Ti amo* (I love you), *scrivo* (I write), or *parlo* (I speak).

Verbs

Italian verbs are a bit more complicated because of the many different conjugations that affect their endings. Because you won't find most conjugated verbs in the dictionary, it is *importante* to listen for the root of the word.

Verb Families

There are three kinds of verb families in Italian, *-are*, *-ere*, and *-ire*. Each family has its own particular way of doing things. All three families of verbs are called *regular* verbs because they prescribe to a given set of consistent rules.

Irregular verbs follow their own rules. See Appendix A for an overview of these verbs.

Conjugating Verbs

To conjugate verbs, drop the infinitive ending from the stem and then add the conjugated endings (in bold). Study the verbs *celebrare* (to celebrate), *scrivere* (to write), *dormire* (to sleep), and *capire* (to understand).

The *-ire* verbs have two forms of conjugation. The *-ere* verbs tend to be highly irregular and often do not conform to the regular rules.

Subject Pronoun	Celebrare	Scrivere	Dormire	Capire
io	celebr-**o**	scriv-**o**	dorm-**o**	cap-**isco**
tu	celebr-**i**	scriv-**i**	dorm-**i**	cap-**isci**
lui, lei, Lei	celebr-**a**	scriv-**e**	dorm-**e**	cap-**isce**
noi	celebr-**iamo**	scriv-**iamo**	dorm-**iamo**	cap-**iamo**
voi	celebr-**ate**	scriv-**ete**	dorm-**ite**	cap-**ite**
loro*	celebr-**ano**	scriv-**ono**	dorm-**ono**	cap-**iscono**

*Verbs conjugated using the subject loro *tend to be emphasized on the third-to-last syllable.*

Cognates: A Bridge Between Languages

Cognates are words that are similar to and look the same as other words in a foreign language. The endings and pronunciation of certain Italian/English cognates may be slightly different, but the words are essentially the same.

You'll see an astounding number of similarities between English and Italian, especially when you begin
looking at the roots of both language systems.

Fake It 'Til You Make It

The following endings generally translate from
English to Italian. (Note that there are always
exceptions to every rule.) By simply changing the
ending, you'll find yourself faking it in no time.

English Ending	Italian Ending	English Example	Italian Example
-ble	-ibile	terrible	terribile
-ence	-enza	patience	pazienza
-ent	-ente	present	presente
-ion	-ione	vision	visione
-ism	-ismo	realism	realismo
-ous	-oso	famous	famoso
-ty	-tà	identity	identità

Beware of False Friends

A *false cognate* is a word in Italian that sounds like
an English word but means something different.
Here are a few false cognates to watch out for:

ape	bee	*come*	how
assumere	to hire	*con*	with
camera	room	*fabbrica*	factory
cane	dog	*fattoria*	farm

caldo	hot	*firma*	signature
caro	expensive	*libreria*	bookstore
coincidenza	connection	*parente*	relative

Things Every *Bambino* Knows

In This Chapter

- Simple phrases
- Days and months
- Weather and climate
- Colors
- Numbers
- Telling time
- Who, what, where, when, and other question words

By now you know that pronouncing Italian is a piece of *torta* (cake—see how it relates to the word *tortellini?*). It's time to learn the basics, what every *bambino* knows, and what you should, too. These are easy things to remember, so you'll build up your communication confidence while developing your *vocabolario*.

Remember your objectives. Personally, I break it down to one thing: communicating your needs. (*Bambini* tend to do so very successfully, or we wouldn't still be here, no?)

Mind Your Manners

Every well-mannered *bambino* learns these helpful expressions almost as soon as he or she can walk. You'll hear the following phrases used often.

English	Italian	Pronunciation
Excuse me.	Mi scusi.	mee skoo-zee
Please.	Per favore.	per fah-**voh**-ray
Please.	Per piacere.	per pee-ah-**cheh**-ray
Thank you.	Grazie.	**grah**-tsee-yay
You're welcome.	Prego.	pray-goh
I'm sorry.	Mi dispiace.	mee dee-spee-**ah**-cheh
May I? Can I?	Posso?	pohs-soh
I would like …	Vorrei …	vohr-**reh**
I want …	Desidero …	deh-**zee**-deh-roh
I need …	Ho bisogno di …	oh bee-**zohn**-yoh dee
I beg you! (informal, particularly useful for whining)	Ti prego!	tee preh-goh
Come on! (informal)	Dai!	dy
Good job!	Bravo/a! (m./f.)	brah-voh/vah

English	Italian	Pronunciation
Ready! Hello!*	Pronto!	pron-toh
Let's go/ we're going.	Andiamo.	ahn-dee-**yah**-moh

*Pronto is used to answer the telephone and goes back to the days when the operator first gathered everyone on the line before connecting the callers.

La Bella Lingua

The informal terms **salve** and **ciao** are used to say "hello" and, more often, "goodbye" almost everywhere in Italy. Also commonly used among friends are the expressions **Ci vediamo** and **A presto!,** equivalent to saying "see you later." **Arrivederci** literally means "to re-see one another." **ArrivederLa** means the same thing but is used under more formal circumstances.

I Giorni della Settimana: Days of the Week

In my *famiglia*, Sunday was always pasta day, and my *padre*—the cook in the family—began stirring the sauce almost as soon as we cleaned up the sugar from the pastries we brought home from church.

You may not have realized, but almost every day corresponds with a planet. For example, *lunedì* corresponds with *la luna*, as in "moon day." Italians have adopted the English way of expressing the end of the week by using the English word *weekend*, but you will also hear *il fine settimana* expressed as well.

Day of the Week	Italian	Pronunciation
Monday	lunedì	loo-neh-**dee**
Tuesday	martedì	mar-teh-**dee**
Wednesday	mercoledì	mer-koh-leh-**dee**
Thursday	giovedì	joh-veh-**dee**
Friday	venerdì	veh-ner-**dee**
Saturday	sabato	**sah**-bah-toh
Sunday	domenica	doh-**meh**-nee-kah
the weekend	il fine settimana	eel fee-neh set-tee-**mah**-nah
	il weekend	same as English

Months

If you're planning your next *viaggio* or want to talk about *l'astrologia*, knowing the month is *importante*. Like the days of the week, the months are not capitalized in Italian.

Month	Mese	Pronunciation
January	gennaio	jeh-**nah**-yoh
February	febbraio	feb-**brah**-yoh
March	marzo	mar-tsoh

Month	Mese	Pronunciation
April	aprile	ahp-**ree**-leh
May	maggio	mahj-joh
June	giugno	joo-nyoh
July	luglio	loo-lyoh
August	agosto	ah-**goh**-stoh
September	settembre	seht-**tem**-breh
October	ottobre	oht-**toh**-breh
November	novembre	noh-**vem**-breh
December	dicembre	dee-**chem**-breh

The seasons are important to know as well:

| spring | *la primavera* | autumn | *l'autunno* |
| summer | *l'estate* | winter | *l'inverno* |

Keep the following rules in mind when talking about dates in Italian:

- Like the days of the week, the months are not capitalized in Italian.
- The month always comes after the day and you must always put the definite article in front of the day. Ditto for abbreviations. Keep this in mind when reading Italian documents. For example, my *compleanno* (birthday, as in "completed year") would look like this:

  June 25, 1965 (6/25/65)

  Il 25 giugno 1965 (25.6.65)

- Ordinal numbers are used for the first day of any month.

  June 1st   *Il primo giugno*

- When pronouncing days of the week, remember to emphasize the last syllable, as indicated by the grave accent (`` ` ``).

Auguri! Best Wishes

Most businesses, banks, and many stores close on holidays. Four-day weekends are not uncommon if a holiday falls on a *giovedì* (Thursday) or *lunedì* (Monday), referred to as *fare il ponte* (making the bridge). Keep this in mind when planning your *vacanza*. If you want to offer someone "good wishes," tell them *Auguri!*

Weather or Not

The weather will determine whether you spend the day outdoors or inside. Talking about *il tempo* (the weather) also makes for lovely small talk.

English	Italian	Pronunciation
What's the weather?	Che tempo fa?	kay tem-poh fah
It's beautiful.	Fa bel tempo.	fah behl-loh
It's hot.	Fa caldo.	fah kahl-doh
It's cold.	Fa freddo.	fah fred-doh
It's bad.	Fa brutto tempo.	fah broo-toh
It's cool.	Fa fresco.	fah freh-skoh

English	Italian	Pronunciation
It's sunny.	C'è sole.	chay soh-leh
It's windy.	C'è vento.	chay ven-toh
It's cloudy.	È nuvoloso.	ay noo-voh-**loh**-zoh
It's humid.	È umido.	ay **oo**-mee-doh
It's raining.	Piove.	pee-**oh**-veh
It's snowing.	Nevica.	**neh**-vee-kah
There is a storm.	C'è un temporale.	chay oon tem-per-ah-leh
What is the temperature today?	Quanto fa oggi?	kwahn-toh fah ohj-jee
It is (30) degrees.*	Fa (trenta) gradi.	fah tren-tah grah-dee

Celsius

Climatic Conditions

There's a lot more out there than rain, sun, and snow. How about snowflakes? Rainbows? Sunsets and sunrises?

English	Italian	English	Italian
air	l'aria	ozone	l'ozono
avalanche	la valanga	mud	il fango
calm	sereno	pollution	l'inquinamento
Celsius	grado centigrade	rain	la pioggia
climate	il clima	rainbow	l'arcobaleno

continues

continued

English	Italian	English	Italian
cloud	la nuvola	rainy	piovoso
cloudy	nuvoloso	smog	lo smog
dry	secco	snow	la neve
frost	la brina	snowflake	il fiocco di neve
humid	umido	sunrise	l'alba
ice	il ghiaccio	sunset	il tramonto
lightning bolt	il fulmine/ il lampo	tropical	tropicale

When in Roma ...

In Italy, as in all of Europe, the metric system is used to determine the temperature. To convert Centigrade to Fahrenheit, multiply the Centigrade temperature by 1.8 and add 32.

To convert Fahrenheit to Centigrade, subtract 32 from the Fahrenheit temperature and multiply the remaining number by .5.

Here are some basic temperature reference points:

Freezing: 32°F = 0°C

Room Temperature: 68°F = 20°C

Body Temperature: 98.6°F = 37°C

Boiling: 212°F = 100°C

Color My *Mondo*

Seeing is believing. One of the first things every *bambino* learns are the *colori*.

English	Italian	Pronunciation
beige	beige	behj
black	nero	neh-roh
blue	blu	bloo
brown	marrone*	mar-**roh**-neh
gold	oro	oh-roh
gray	grigio	gree-joh
green	verde	ver-deh
orange	arancione	ah-rahn-**choh**-neh
pink	rosa	roh-zah
purple	viola	vee-**oh**-lah
red	rosso	rohs-soh
silver	argento	ar-**jen**-toh
sky blue	azzurro	ah-**tsoor**-roh
white	bianco	bee-**ahn**-koh
yellow	giallo	jahl-loh

*Marrone *is a false cognate and means* "brown," *not* maroon.

Counting with Numbers

Uno, due, tre … Numbers are easy in Italian. Since the euro replaced lire, accounting in Italian is a walk in the park.

English	Italian	Pronunciation
0	zero	zeh-roh
1	uno	oo-noh
2	due	doo-eh
3	tre	treh
4	quattro	kwaht-troh
5	cinque	cheen-kweh
6	sei	say
7	sette	seht-teh
8	otto	oht-toh
9	nove	noh-veh
10	dieci	dee-**ay**-chee
11	undici	**oon**-dee-chee
12	dodici	**doh**-dee-chee
13	tredici	**treh**-dee-chee
14	quattordici	kwaht-**tor**-dee-chee
15	quindici	**kween**-dee-chee
16	sedici	**say**-dee-chee
17	diciassette	dee-chah-**seht**-teh
18	diciotto	dee-**choht**-toh
19	diciannove	dee-chahn-**noh**-veh
20	venti	ven-tee
21	ventuno	ven-**too**-noh
22	ventidue	ven-tee-**doo**-weh
23	ventitrè	ven-tee-**treh**
24	ventiquattro	ven-tee-**kwaht**-troh
25	venticinque	ven-tee-**cheen**-kweh
26	ventisei	ven-tee-**say**
27	ventisette	ven-tee-**seht**-teh

English	Italian	Pronunciation
28	ventotto	ven-**toht**-toh
29	ventinove	ven-tee-**noh**-veh
30	trenta	tren-tah
40	quaranta	kwah-**rahn**-tah
50	cinquanta	cheen-**kwahn**-tah
60	sessanta	sehs-**sahn**-tah
70	settanta	seht-**tahn**-tah
80	ottanta	oht-**tahn**-tah
90	novanta	noh-**vahn**-tah
100	cento	chen-toh
101	centuno	chen-**too**-noh
200	duecento	doo-ay-**chen**-toh
300	trecento	treh-**chen**-toh
400	quattrocento	kwaht-troh-**chen**-toh
500	cinquecento	cheen-kway-**chen**-toh
1.000	mille	meel-leh
1.001	milleuno	meel-leh-**oo**-noh
1.200	milleduecento	meel-leh-doo-eh-**chen**-toh
2.000	duemila	doo-eh-**mee**-lah
3.000	tremila	treh-**mee**-lah
10.000	diecimila	dee-ay-chee-**mee**-lah
20.000	ventimila	ven-tee-**mee**-lah
100.000	centomila	chen-toh-**mee**-lah
200.000	duecentomila	doo-eh-chen-toh-**mee**-lah
1.000.000	un milione	oon mee-**lyoh**-neh
1.000.000.000	un miliardo	oon mee-**lyar**-doh

Keep in mind these brief notes on writing numbers in Italian:

- Italian uses a period to indicate units of thousands.

English	Italian
2,000	2.000

- In Italian, you must use commas in decimal numbers. It is read as *e* (and):

English	Italian
1.25	1,25

La Bella Lingua

Numbers under 100 ending in a vowel, such as *venti* (20), drop the vowel when connected to secondary numbers. Examples include *ventuno* (21), *trentotto* (38), *quarantuno* (41), etc.

After the number *mille* (1,000), *mila* is used in the plural, as in, *due mila* (2,000).

Che Ora è? Telling Time

The following table spells out how to tell the time minute by minute, hour by hour. Italian schedules tend to be in military time, so you'll want to be able to count to *ventiquattro* (24).

English	Italian
What time is it?	Che ora è? Che ore sono?
It is noon.	È mezzogiorno.
It is midnight.	È mezzanotte.
It is bedtime.	È l'ora di dormire.
It is 1:00.	È l'una.
It is 2:00.	Sono le due.
It is 2:05.	Sono le due e cinque.
It is 3:10.	Sono le tre e dieci.
It is 4:15.	Sono le quattro e un quarto.
It is 5:20.	Sono le cinque e venti.
It is 6:25.	Sono le sei e venticinque.
It is 6:30.	Sono le sei e trenta.
It is 8:40. (20 min. to 9)	Sono le nove meno venti.
It is 9:45. (quarter to 10)	Sono le dieci meno un quarto.
It is 10:50. (10 min. to 11)	Sono le undici meno dieci.
It is 11:55. (5 min. to noon)	È mezzogiorno meno cinque.

When in Roma ...

Be careful of the Italian word *tempo*, used for both the weather (as in *temperatura*) and time.

Che tempo fa?   What's the weather?

Non ho tempo.   I don't have time.

The Quest for Knowledge: Questions and Answers

To ask a question in Italian, just raise your voice at the end of any phrase, just like you would do in English. There's no need to change the word order. However, the problem is usually not asking the question, it's understanding the answer that can often cause *confusione*. *Bambini* ask a lot of questions, especially *perché* (why?) and *quando* (when?). With a few hand gestures, you should be able to get the gist of things in no time.

English	Italian	Pronunciation
Do you speak English?	Parla inglese?	par-lah een-**gleh**-zeh
I don't understand.	Non capisco.	nohn kah-**pee**-skoh
Can you repeat that again?	Può ripetere di nuovo?	pwoh ree-**peh**-teh-reh dee nwoh-voh
What does it mean?	Che significa?	kay see-**gnee**-fee-kah
How do you say …?	Come si dice …?	koh-meh see dee-chay
How much does it cost?	Quanto costa?	kwahn-toh kohs-tah
How	Come	koh-meh
What	Che cosa*	kay koh-zah
When	Quando	kwahn-doh
Where	Dove	doh-veh
Where is …?	Dov'è …?	doh-**vay**
Who is he/she?	Chi è?	kee **ay**
Why	perché	per-**kay**

*Che cosa *(what) can also be broken down to either word,* che *and* cosa. Cosa *additionally translates to mean "thing."*

Chapter 3

Friends and *Famiglia*

In This Chapter

- Basic greetings and other pleasantries
- Introductions
- Family members
- Professions
- Expressions for "being" and "having"

This chapter gives you the vocabulary to say hello and goodbye. It will also help you to describe you and your family, who you are, and what you do.

It also offers you three essential verbs—*essere, stare,* and *avere*—that will help you express yourself in countless ways.

Buon Giorno! Basic Italian Greetings and Other Common Exchanges

Many roads lead to Roma. Use these helpful phrases anywhere you go. *Buona avventura!*

English	Italian	Pronunciation
Hello; good day.	Buon giorno.	bwon jor-noh
Good evening.	Buona sera.	bwoh-nah seh-rah
Good night/ Goodbye.	Buona notte.	bwoh-nah not-teh
Goodbye.	ArrivederLa.	ah-ree-veh-**der**-lah
Mr./Sir	Signore	see-**nyoh**-reh
Mrs./Ms.	Signora	see-**nyoh**-rah
Miss	Signorina	see-nyoh-**ree**-nah
How are you?	Come sta?	koh-meh stah
Very well.	Molto bene.	mohl-toh beh-neh
Not bad.	Non c'è male.	nohn chay mah-leh
Pretty well.	Abbastanza bene.	ah-bah-**stahn**-zah beh-neh
What is your name?*	Come si chiama?	koh-meh see kee-**ah**-mah
My name is … (I call myself)	Mi chiamo …	mee kee-**ah**-moh
See you soon.	A presto.	ah preh-stoh
Excuse me.	Mi scusi.	mee skoo-zee
Please.	Per favore.	per fah-**voh**-reh
Please.	Per piacere.	per pee-ah-**cheh**-reh
Thank you.	Grazie.	**grah**-tsee-yay
You are welcome.	Prego.	pray-goh
You are welcome. (It's nothing.)	Non c'è di che.	nohn chay dee kay
You are very kind.	Lei è molto gentile.	leh eh mohl-toh jen-**tee**-leh

*(How do you call yourself?)

After you've had the opportunity to get to know someone a little better, you can use these informal greetings.

English	Italian	Pronunciation
Hi/Bye-bye!	Ciao!	chow
Greetings!	Saluti!	sah-**loo**-tee
How are you?	Come stai?	koh-meh sty
Hello!	Salve!	sal-veh
How's it going?	Come va?	koh-meh vah
Things are good.	Va bene.	vah beh-neh
Not so good.	Va male.	vah mah-leh
Not bad.	Non c'è male.	nohn chay mah-leh
So-so.	Così così.	koh-**zee** koh-**zee**
See you later.	Arrivederci.	ah-ree-veh-**der**-chee
Until later.	A più tardi.	ah pyoo tar-dee
Until tomorrow.	A domani.	ah doh-**mah**-nee

Blood Is Thicker Than Water: Your Family

In Italy, one of the first things people will want to know about is your *famiglia* (pronounced fah-**mee**-lyah).

Substitute the word in parentheses with the appropriate term. Notice that the possessive adjective changes depending on the gender of the thing or person being possessed. Useful phrases include the following:

Feminine:	*Questa è mia (moglie).*	This is my (wife).	
Masculine:	*Questo è mio (marito).*	This is my (husband).	

La Bella Lingua

When discussing one's "children" of both sexes, Italian reverts to the masculine plural: *figli*. The same goes for friends: *amici*. One's *genitori* (parents) can be simply referred to as *i miei*, coming from the possessive adjective "my" as in "my parents."

Feminine	Italian	Masculine	Italian
aunt	zia	uncle	zio
cousin	cugina	cousin	cugino
daughter	figlia	son	figlio
daughter-in-law	nuora	son-in-law	genero
fiancée	fidanzata	fiancé	fidanzato
friend	amica	friend	amico
girlfriend	ragazza	boyfriend	ragazzo
godmother	madrina	godfather	padrino
granddaughter	nipote	grandson	nipote
grandmother	nonna	grandfather	nonno
infant	bambina	infant	bambino
mother	madre	father	padre
mother-in-law	suocera	father-in-law	suocero

Feminine	Italian	Masculine	Italian
niece	nipote	nephew	nipote
sister	sorella	brother	fratello
sister-in-law	cognata	brother-in-law	cognato
stepsister	sorellastra	stepbrother	fratellastro
wife	moglie	husband	marito
widow	vedova	widower	vedovo

Attenzione!

Always remember to emphasize double consonants while making sure you pronounce them as one single sound. For example: *mamma* (mahm-mah).

Professioni (Professions)

What do you profess to be? Helpful phrases include the following:

Sono	(I am) …
Che professione fa?	(What profession do you do?)

English	Italian	English	Italian
accountant	contabile	hairdresser	parrucchiere
actor	attore	housewife	casalinga
analyst	analista	lawyer	avvocato
architect	architetto	manager	amministratore
artist	artista	mechanic	meccanico
assistant	assistente	merchant	commerciante
banker	bancario	musician	musicista
barber	barbiere	nurse	infermiera
cashier	cassiere	photographer	fotografo
chef	cuoco	plumber	idraulico
consultant	consulente	police officer	vigile
dentist	dentista	scientist	scienziato
doctor	dottore/ dottoressa	secretary	segretaria
driver	autista	student	studente/ studentessa
electrician	elettricista	teacher	insegnante
farmer	agricoltore	waiter	cameriere

What's What

When referring to a feminine subject, unless otherwise indicated, you must change the ending (which is by default masculine) to an *-a*. For example, *scienziato* signifies a male scientist, whereas *scienziata* would refer to a female scientist. Of course, a scientist is a scientist, regardless the gender of the person doing the thinking.

Useful Verbiage: Being

The Italian verbs *essere* (to be) and *stare* (to be; to stay) can help you enormously in your communications. You'll hear these used often.

Subject Pronouns	Essere	Stare	Meaning
io	sono	sto	I am
tu	sei	stai	you are (familiar)
lui/lei/Lei	è	sta	he/she is; You are
noi	siamo	stiamo	we are
voi	siete	state	you are
loro	sono	stanno	they are

Refer to Appendix A for a practical summary of Italian verbs.

When to Use *Essere*

- To describe nationalities, origins, and inherent unchanging qualities:

Maurizio è di Verona.	Maurizio is from Verona.
Siamo Italiani.	We are Italians.
La banana è gialla.	The banana is yellow.

- To identify the subject or describe the subject's character traits:

Voi siete gentili.	You all are kind.
Michele è un musicista.	Michael is a musician.
Sono io.	It's me.

- To talk about the time and dates:

  Che ore sono?   What time is it?

  Che giorno è?   What day is it?

- To indicate possession:

  Questa è la zia di Anna. This is Anna's aunt.

  Quella è la mia casa.   That is my house.

When to Use *Stare*

- To describe a temporary state or condition of the subject:

  Come sta?   How are you?

  Sto bene, grazie.   I am well, thanks.

- To express location:

  Stiamo in città.   We are staying in the city.

  Patrizia sta a casa.   Patricia is at home.

- In many idiomatic expressions:

  Sta' attento!   Pay attention!

  Sta' zitto!   Be quiet!

Avere: To Have

You'll get a lot of mileage using the verb *avere*. Keep in mind that the *h* is always silent.

Subject Pronouns	Avere	Meaning
io	ho	I have
tu	hai	you have (familiar)
lui/lei/Lei	ha	he/she has; You have
noi	abbiamo	we have
voi	avete	you have
loro	hanno	they have

Useful idiomatic expressions include the following:

Quanti anni ha?	How old are you? (How many years do you have?)
Ho (venticinque) anni.	I am (twenty-five) years old.
Ho freddo/caldo.	I am cold/warm.
Abbiamo fretta.	We are in a rush.

Chapter 4

Buon Viaggio: Getting Around

In This Chapter

- Airport expressions
- Asking for directions
- Buses and trains and other modes of transportation
- Making the connection
- Taxis
- Other useful travel-related verbiage

This chapter gives you the vocabulary you need to get around. Most likely, you'll still get lost; if you consider it all part of the *avventura*, however, you'll enjoy the ride a whole lot more!

At the Airport

Chances are, airline personnel will speak English at the airport. But just in case, here are all of the terms you need to maneuver through the airport and onto your plane.

English	Italian	English	Italian
customs	la dogana	emergency exit	l'uscita d'emergenza
on board	a bordo	flight	il volo
porter	un porta-bagagli; un facchino	flight attendant	l'assistente di volo
airline	la linea aerea	gate	il cancello
the airplane	l'aeroplano	information	le informazioni
the airport	l'aereoporto	landing	l'atterraggio
aisle	il corridoio	life vest	il giubbotto di salvataggio
arrival	l'arrivo	lost and found	l'ufficio oggetti smarriti
arrival time	l'ora d'arrivo	money exchange	il cambio
baggage	i bagagli	reservation	la preno-tazione
baggage claim	la riconsegna/ il ritiro bagagli	row	la fila
car rental	l'autonoleggio	seat	il posto
cart	il carrello	seat belt	la cintura di sicurezza
connection	la coincidenza	take-off	il decollo
departure	la partenza	ticket	il biglietto
departure time	l'ora di partenza	trip	il viaggio
destination	la destinazione	window	il finestrino
elevator	l'ascensore		

What's What

Your comprehension will be facilitated if you keep in mind that all Italian nouns require an article in front of them. For example, *l'ora d'arrivo* (loh-rah dar-ree-**voh**) translates to "the hour of arrival." Refer back to Chapter 1 for a brief summary of your articles.

Go the extra kilometer. Helpful airport-related expressions include the following:

English	Italian	Pronunciation
Where is customs?	Dov'è la dogana?	doh-**vay** lah doh-**gah**-nah
I have nothing to declare.	Non ho niente da dichiarare.	nohn oh nee-**yen**-teh dah dee-kee-**yah**-reh
I'd like a seat near the window/aisle.	Vorrei un posto vicino al finestrino/corridoio.	vohr-**reh** oon poh-stoh vee-**chee**-noh ahl fee-neh-**stree**-noh/cor-ree-**doy**-oh
I'd like to travel in first/second class.	Vorrei viaggiare in prima/seconda classe.	vohr-**reh** vee-ahj-**jah**-reh een pree-mah/seh-**kohn**-dah klahs-seh
I'd like to reserve a place.	Vorrei prenotare un posto.	vohr-**reh** preh-noh-**tah**-reh oon poh-stoh

Asking for Directions

The most basic expressions you can use are *Dov'è ...?* (Where is ...?) and *C'è ...?* (Is there ...?). If you think you've understood, don't just nod like an idiot, say: *Ho capito* (oh kah-**pee**-toh), which means "I have understood." If not, say *Non ho capito* (nohn oh kah-**pee**-toh).

> **La Bella Lingua** _____
>
> When asking for *indicazioni*, stick with simple questions that allow for simple responses. Useful phrases and vocabulary include the following:
>
> | | |
> |---|---|
> | *C'è ...?* | Is there ...? |
> | *Ci sono ...?* | Are there ...? |
> | *Dov'è ...?* | Where is ...? |
> | *Sinistra/Destra* | Left/Right |
> | *Dritto* | Straight |

How Do I Get to ...?

When you're on foot, sometimes the best thing to do is point to your map and raise your eyebrows. You may hear or want to use these commands (always given in the polite form of the verb) and phrases to help you along your way.

English	Italian	Pronunciation
At the corner	all'angolo	ahl-**lan**-goh-loh
At the intersection	all'incrocio	ah-leen-**kroh**-choh
At the stop sign	allo stop	ahl-loh stop
At the traffic light	al semaforo	ahl seh-mah-**foh**-roh
Can I get there by foot?	Posso andarci a piedi?	pohs-soh ahn-**dar**-chee ah pee-**yeh**-dee
Can you please repeat that?	Me lo ripeti per favore?	me loh ree-**peh**-tee per fah-**voh**-reh
Can you tell me how to get to …?	Mi può dire come arrivare a …?	me pwoh dee-reh koh-meh ar-ree-**vah**-reh ah
Can you indicate where centro* is?	Mi può indicare dov'è il centro?	me pwoh een-dee-**kah**-reh doh-**vay** eel chen-troh
Can you tell me …?	Sa dirmi …?	sah deer-me
Cross	Attraversi	aht-trah-**ver**-see
Down at the end (of the street)	giù in fondo.	joo een fon-doh
Further on	più avanti	pyoo ah-**vahn**-tee
Go down/get off.	Scenda	shen-dah
Go straight ahead.	Vada sempre dritto.	vah-dah semp-reh dree-toh
Go up/get on.	Salga.	sal-gah
Here/There	qui;qua/lì;là	kwee;kwah/lee;lah
I'm lost.	Mi sono perso.	me soh-noh per-soh
It is far/near.	È lontano/ vicino.	**ay** lon-tah-noh/ vee-**chee**-noh
Take this street.	Prenda questa strada.	pren-dah kweh-stah strah-dah
Turn around.	Torni indietro.	tor-nee een-dee-**yeh**-troh

continues

continued

English	Italian	Pronunciation
Turn left/right.	Giri a sinistra/ a destra.	jee-ree ah see-**nee**-strah/ah des-trah
We're looking for centro*.	Il cerchiamo il centro.	eel cher-kee-**yah**-moh eel chen-troh
What street are you looking for?	Che strada cerca?/	kay strah-dah cher-kah
	Che strada sta cercando?	kay strah-dah stah cher-**kahn**-doh

*Centro *is the generic term used for "downtown"—usually where you'll find most of the action in any* città.

Things That Go: Modes of Transportation

Andiamo! Let's go! The following list of *mezzi di trasporto* (modes of transportation) will get you somewhere other than here.

English	Italian	English	Italian
by bus	in autobus	by ferry	in traghetto
by bicycle	in bicicletta	by subway	in metropolitana
by car	in automobile	by taxi	in tassì
by car	in macchina	by train	in treno

When in Roma ...

All roads lead to Roma. To make sure you're on track, the following all signify "road" in some form or another:

la via	the street
la strada	the road
la strada non asfaltata	the dirt road
il viale	the avenue
l'autostrada	the highway
l'autostrada a pedaggio	the turnpike

If You're Going by Train or Bus

It's a good idea to purchase bus tickets at a *cartoleria* (stationary store) or *tabacchi* (tobacco store) to keep in your wallet. (City buses do not accept cash or coins.) You can also buy *biglietti* (tickets) at train stations and from automated machines. When you get onto *l'autobus,* you must validate your ticket with the time and date by punching the ticket into the small metal box usually affixed to a pole near the center of the bus.

Whether you are traveling by *autobus* or *treno,* you'll need to know the following vocabulary.

English	Italian	English	Italian
connection	la coincidenza	the ticket counter	la biglietteria
first/second class	di prima/ seconda classe	the ticket office	l'ufficio biglietti

continues

continued

English	Italian	English	Italian
one-way	di andata	the track	il binario
round-trip	di andata e ritorno	the train	il treno
the last stop/ end of the line	il capolinea	the train station	la stazione ferroviaria
the railway	la ferrovia	the waiting room	la sala d'aspetto
the schedule	l'orario	the restaurant car	il vagone ristorante
the stop	la fermata	the sleeping car	il vagone letto
the ticket	il biglietto		

What's What

In Italian, *direzioni* refer to the poles. Keep in mind that most Italians follow the highways from town to town, as you'll see when confronted with the names of 12 cities and just as many arrows pointing you in opposite directions.

north	*nord*	east	*est*
south	*sud*	west	*ovest*

If You're Going by *Tassì* (Taxi)

Italians use the words *tassì* and *taxi* interchangeably. Use the following expressions to tell where you are and where you want to go.

English	Italian	Pronunciation
Where is the nearest taxi stand?	Dov'è il posteggio dei tassì più vicino?	doh-**vay** eel poh-**stej**-joh dee tas-**see** pyoo vee-**chee**-noh
I need a taxi.	Ho bisogno di un tassì.	oh bee-**zoh**-nyoh dee oon tas-**see**
I'd like to go	Vorrei andare	vor-**reh** ahn-**dah**-reh
Stop here.	Si fermi qui.	see fer-mee kwee
Please wait for me.	Mi aspetti, per favore.	mee ah-**spet**-tee per fah-**voh**-reh

Making the Trip

Save yourself time and trouble: ask questions. Useful phrases and questions related to travel include the following:

English	Italian	Pronunciation
How many kilometers to Narni from here?	Quanti chilometri dista Narni da qui?	kwahn-tee kee-**loh**-meh-tree dee-stah nar-nee dah kwee
How much does it cost?	Quanto costa?	kwahn-toh koh-stah
I would like a round-trip ticket to Florence.	Vorrei un biglietto di andata e ritorno per Firenze.	vohr-**reh** oon bee-**lyet**-toh dee ahn-**dah**-tah eh ree-**tor**-noh per fee-**ren**-zeh
I'd like a seat next to the window.	Vorrei un posto accanto al finestrino.	vohr-**reh** oon poh-stoh ahk-**kan**-toh ahl fee-neh-**stree**-noh

continues

continued

English	Italian	Pronunciation
I'd like to reserve a seat.	Vorrei prenotare un posto.	vohr-**reh** preh-noh-**tah**-reh oon poh-stoh
Is (it) on time/late?	È in orario/ritardo?	**ay** een oh-**rah**-ryoh/ree-**tar**-doh
Is it close?	È vicino?	ay vee-**chee**-noh
Is it far?	È lontano?	ay lon-**tah**-noh
Is there a connection?	C'è la coincidenza?	**chay** lah koh-een-chee-**den**-zah
On what track does the train leave?	Su quale binario parte il treno?	su kwah-leh bee-**nah**-ree-yoh par-teh eel treh-noh
We're going to Rome.	Andiamo a Roma.	ahn-dee-**yah**-moh ah roh-mah
We're lost.	Ci siamo persi.	chee see-**yah**-moh per-see
What time does the train/bus leave for …?	A che ora parte il treno/l'autobus per …?	ah kay oh-rah par-teh eel treh-noh/**lao**-toh-boos
When does (it) leave/arrive?	Quando parte/arriva?	kwahn-doh par-teh/ar-**ree**-vah
Where is the bus stop?	Dov'è la fermata dell'autobus?	doh-**vay** lah fer-**mah**-tah deh-**lao**-toh-boos
Where is the waiting room?	Dov'è la sala d'aspetto?	doh-**vay** lah sah-lah dah-**spet**-toh

Useful Travel Verbs and Expressions

For the more adventuresome (linguistically, that is), I've included some commonly used travel-related verbs that may come in handy. Refer back to Chapter 3 for a review of the verb *essere* (to be).

English	Italian	English	Italian
to be early	essere in anticipo	to go down/ to get off	scendere
to be late	essere in ritardo	to go up/ to get on	salire
to be on time	essere in orario	to leave	partire
to board	imbarcare	to lose	perdere
to change	cambiare	to return	ritornare/ tornare
to come	venire	to take	prendere
to commute	fare il pendolare	to turn	girare
to go	andare		

Chapter 5

Drive Like the Italians

In This Chapter

- Renting a car
- Driving lingo
- Parking
- Road signs
- Car breakdowns and accidents

Just because you're in Italy doesn't give you license to drive like a maniac. I trust you road runners will drive responsibly.

Renting a Car

You'll often find better rates if you reserve a car from home rather than renting directly from the airport. Be sure to ask about specials, especially during the off-season when there is less demand. And always check a rental car *before* you drive away for existing scratches, dents, or damage so you won't be charged for them when you return the car.

What's What

Italian adjectives reflect the gender of the subject. Adjectives ending in -o should be changed to -a when the subject of the verb is feminine.

English	Italian	Pronunciation
How much does automobile insurance cost?	Quanto costa l'assicurazione per l'auto?	kwahn-toh koh-stah lahs-see-koo-rah-tsee-**oh**-neh per lao-toh
How much does it cost per day (per week) (per kilometer)?	Quanto costa al giorno (alla settimana) (al chilometro)?	kwahn-toh koh-stah ahl jor-noh (ah-lah set-tee-**mah**-nah) (ahl kee-**loh**-meh-troh
I'd like to rent a car (with automatic transmission).	Vorrei noleggiare una macchina (con il cambio auto-matico)	vohr-**reh** noh-lehj-**jah**-reh oo-nah **mahk**-kee-nah (kohn eel **kahm**-bee-oh ow-toh-**mah**-tee-koh)
There's some damage.	C'è un guasto.	chay oon gwah-stoh

Car Talk

A few words of advice: Remember to stay in the right lane unless you're passing someone. Contrary to popular belief, Italian *autostrade* do have speeding limits. Watch out for motorcycles and *vespas*, much more common in Italy due to the higher prices of gas. Make sure you know whether your car requires *benzina* (the European equivalent to gasoline) or diesel before you need to gas up.

When traveling to Italy, your valid U.S. driver's license will do. Discounts off the price of a rental are often made available to drivers in possession of an international driver's license. Call your local AAA office for more details. *P.S.* Almost all European rental cars are stick-shift; you need to specifically ask for an automatic transmission car if you don't know how to drive a manual transmission.

The following table provides you with all the car talk you may require.

English	Italian	English	Italian
accelerator	l'acceleratore	license	la patente
air conditioning	l'aria condizionata	license plate	la targa
battery	la batteria	muffler	la marmitta
brakes	i freni	oil	l'olio
carburetor	il carburatore	radiator	la radiatore
door handle	la maniglia	radio	la radio
engine; motor	il motore	rear-view mirror	lo specchietto retrovisore
fan belt	la cinghia del ventilatore	sign	il segnale
fender	il parafango	spark plug	la candela d'accensione
flat tire	una gomma; una ruota a terra	speed limit	il limite di velocità
gas tank	il serbatoio	speedometer	il tachimetro

continues

continued

English	Italian	English	Italian
gear stick	il cambio	steering wheel	il volante
glove compartment	il croscompartimento	tail light	la luce di posizione
handbrake	il freno a mano	tire	la ruota
headlights	i fari	trunk	il bagagliaio
hood	il cofano	turn signals	le frecce
horn	il clacson	water	l'acqua
ignition	l'accensione	window	il finestrino
keys	le chiavi	windshield wiper	il tergicristallo

If you've decided to rent *una macchina*, carefully inspect it inside and out. Make sure there is *un cricco* (a jack) and *una ruota di scorta* (a spare tire) in the trunk, in case you get a *gomma a terra* (flat tire).

On the Road

More important than the names of car parts are the instructions, directions, and communications that you'll have to deal with while you're on the road. Refer back to Chapter 4 for a refresher on how to ask for directions.

English	Italian	Pronunciation
traffic officer	il vigile/la vigilessa	eel **vee**-jeh-leh/lah vee-jee-**les**-sah
This car is a rental.	Questa macchina è in affitto.	kweh-stah **mahk**-kee-nah ay een ahf-**fee**-toh

English	Italian	Pronunciation
Can you show me on the map where I am?	Mi può indicare dove sono sulla mappa?	me pwoh een-dee-**kah**-reh doh-veh soh-noh sool-lah mahp-pah
Follow me.	Mi segua.	mee seh-gwah
How do I find this address?	Come posso arrivare a quest'indirizzo?	koh-meh pohs-soh ahr-ree-**vah**-reh ah kwest-een-dee-**ree** tsoh
How many kilometers to ...?	Quanti chilometri dista ...? A quanti chilometri é ...?	kwahn-tee kee-**loh**-meh-tree dee-stah ah kwahn-tee kee-**loh**-meh-tree ay
How do I get to ...?	Come arrivo a ...?	koh-meh ahr-**ree**-voh ah
Is this the correct road for ...?	È questa la strada per ...?	ay kweh-stah lah strah-dah per
Is there traffic?	C'è traffico?	chay **trahf**-fee-koh
In which direction is ...?	In quale direzione è ...?	ecn kwah-leh dee-reh-tsee-**oh**-neh ay

When in Roma ...

In Italy, all roads do—in fact—lead to Rome. Italy's major *autostrada* (highway) is a toll road called the A1 (ah oo-no), which runs the length of the peninsula. When taking this road, you're either going *nord* (north) or *sud* (south). Make sure you have change for the *pedaggio* (toll) when you find your *uscita* (exit).

Parking

Wherever you park—especially in cities—look around for parking meters that require you to pre-pay when parking on the streets and piazzas. The meter will ask you to indicate how long you'll require parking and spit out a small *scontrino* (receipt) after you've pumped in the appropriate euro. This *scontrino* should be placed inside the car on the dashboard and be visible from the outside. You might want to keep some change handy so that you're not left scrambling for coinage when you could be enjoying the sights!

English	Italian	Pronunciation
Where can I park?	Dove posso parcheggiare?	doh-veh pohs-soh par-kehj-**jah**-reh
Is here good?	Va bene qui?	vah beh-neh kwee
Is my car safe?	La macchina è al sicuro?	lah **mahk**-kee-nah ay ahl see-**koo**-roh
Is there a parking meter?	C'è un parcheggio a pagamento?	chay oon par-**kehj**-joh ah pah-gah-**men**-toh
How much per hour?	Quanto costa all'ora?	kwahn-toh koh-stah ahl-**loh**-rah

Signage

You'll encounter the following postings on signs as you make your way through Italy:

Deviazione	Detour
Divieto di ingresso	No Entrance
Divieto di sorpasso	No Passing
Divieto di sosta	No Parking
Sosta autorizzata	Parking Permitted
Doppio senso	Two-Way Traffic
Senso unico	One-Way Traffic

Breakdowns, Accidents, and Other Bummers

It happens. Hopefully you'll avoid accidents by staying attentive and watching what others are doing on the road. In the event things don't go according to plan, the following phrases and vocabulary will enable you to summon help.

English	Italian	Pronunciation
Can you change a tire?	Mi può cambiare la ruota?	mee pwoh kam-bee-**ah**-reh
Can you send a tow truck, please?	Può mandare un carro attrezzi per favore?	pwoh man-**dah**-reh oon kar-roh aht-**treh**-tsee per fah-**voh**-reh
Can you tell me where the nearest mechanic is?	Mi può indicare dov'è il meccanico più vicino?	mee pwoh een-dee-**kah**-reh doh-**vay** eel mek-**kah**-nee-koh pyoo vee-**chee**-noh
Help!	Aiuto!	eye-**yoo**-toh
Here is my license.	Ecco la mia patente.	ek-koh lah mee-yah pah-**ten**-teh
Here is my registration card.	Ecco i documenti della macchina.	ek-koh ee doh-koo-**men**-tee del-lah **mahk**-kee-nah
How long will the repairs take?	Quanto tempo ci vuole per aggiustare la macchina?	kwahn-toh tem-poh chee vwoh-leh per ahj-joo-**stah**-reh lah **mahk**-kee-nah
I am (he/she is) hurt.	Sono (è) ferito.*	soh-noh (ay) feh-**ree**-toh
I've lost the keys.	Ho perso le chiavi.	oh per-soh leh kee-**ah**-vee

English	Italian	Pronunciation
My car has broke down.	La macchina è guasta.	lah **mahk**-kee-nah ay gwah-stah
My car won't start.	La macchina non si mette in moto.	lah **mahk**-kee-nah nohn see met-teh een moh-toh
Please call an ambulance.	Chiami un'ambulanza per favore.	kee-**ah**-mee oon-am-boo-**lahn**-zah per fah-**voh**-reh
Please call the police.	Telefoni la polizia per favore.	teh-**leh**-foh-nee lah poh-lee-**tsee**-ah per fah-**voh**-reh
Please write down your name and address.	Per favore scriva il suo nome e indirizzo.	per fah-**voh**-reh skree-vah eel soo-oh noh-meh eh een-dee-**ree**-tsoh
The car has a flat tire.	La macchina ha una gomma a terra.	lah **mahk**-kee-nah ah oo-nah gohm-mah a ter-rah
The car needs oil/water.	La macchina ha bisogno dell'olio/dell'acqua.	lah **mahk**-kee-nah ah bee-**zoh**-nyoh deh-**loh**-lyoh/del-**lah**-kwah
There's been an accident.	C'è stato un'incidente.	chay stah-toh oon-een-chee-**den**-teh
What an imbecile!	Che imbecille!	kay eem-beh-**chee**-leh
What is your insurance company?	Qual'è la sua assicurazione automobilistica?	kwahl-**ay** lah soo-ah ahs-see-koo-rah-tsee-**oh**-neh ow-toh-moh-bee-**lee**-stee-kah
When will it be ready?	Quando sarà pronta?	kwahn-doh sah-**rah** pron-tah

Feminine: ferita

Useful Travel Verbiage

The following verbs and phrases are given in their unconjugated forms. However, in a pinch, they'll serve you well.

English	Italian	English	Italian
to be prohibited	essere vietato; essere proibito	to give a ride	dare un passaggio
to break down	guastare	to leave	partire
to change a tire	cambiare la ruota	to obey traffic signs	rispettare i segnali stradali
to check	controllare	to park	parcheggiare
to drive	guidare	to return	ritornare; tornare
to get a ticket	prendere una multa	to run out of gas	rimanere senza benzina
to get on	salire su	to run/ function	funzionare
to get off	scendere da	to turn around	tornare indietro

La Bella Lingua

Tools are the last thing you think of when you are planning your trip, but if you're stranded, make sure you have a telephone card along with the following:

hammer	*il martello*
flashlight	*la torcia*
jumper cables	*i cavi con morsetti*
monkey wrench	*la chiave inglese*
pliers	*le pinze*
screwdriver	*il cacciavite*

Chapter 6

Up at the Villa: Lodging

In This Chapter

- Around the hotel
- Types of lodging
- Check-in and check-out
- Expressing your needs
- Housekeeping phrases

If you're staying in a hotel, chances are the staff speak enough English to assist you. If you're in an *agriturismo* (bed and breakfast), you'll need to be flexible and communicate your needs in Italian. That's where I come in.

The Hotel and Nearby

Location is everything. Perhaps you want your hotel to be in the heart of the city, close to the action. Maybe you want a place that is slightly off the beaten track. What services are nearby?

When you check out, you will be given a *fattura* (invoice), *conto* (bill), or *ricevuta* (receipt). Take your receipts: Italian law requires it.

Facilities	Italian	Pronunciation
bar	il bar	eel bar
barber	il barbiere	eel bar-bee-**yeh**-reh
cashier	il cassiere	eel kahs-see-**yeh**-reh
doorman/ concierge	il portiere	eel por-tee-**yeh**-reh
dry-cleaner	la tintoria	lah teen-toh-**ree**-ah
gift shop	il negozio di regali	eel neh-**goh**-zee-oh dee reh-**gah**-lee
gym	la palestra	lah pah-**leh**-strah
hairdresser	il parrucchiere/ la parrucchiera	eel par-rook-kee-**yeh**-reh/lah par-rook-kee-**yeh**-rah
hotel	l'albergo	lahl-**ber**-goh
laundry service	la lavanderia	lah lah-vahn-deh-**ree**-yah
maid	la cameriera	lah kah-meh-ree-**yeh**-rah
parking	il parcheggio	eel par-**kej**-joh
room service	il servizio in camera	eel ser-**vee**-zee-oh een **kah**-meh-rah
swimming pool	la piscina	lah pee-**shee**-nah
tailor	la sartoria	lah sar-toh-**ree**-yah

When in Roma ...

Italy has few Laundromats. Generally, you must give your laundry to the hotel or bring it to a *lavanderia* where it will be cleaned and pressed for you. Usually you pay per piece and not by weight. If you want something dry-cleaned, you must bring it to the *tintoria*.

Making Requests

You may not always get what you want, but hopefully you'll get what you need. The following simple phrases ought to help you ask for what you need. All three expressions can be used interchangeably.

English	Italian	Pronunciation
I would like	Vorrei	vohr-**reh**
I need	Ho bisogno di	oh bee-**zoh**-nyoh dee
I need	Mi serve	me ser-veh

Reserving Your Room

If you're traveling with someone, make sure you reserve a room suited to your needs. Do you need two single beds or one big one?

Amenity	Italian	Pronunciation
I'd like ...	Vorrei ...	vohr-**reh**
a room	una stanza, una camera	oo-nah stan-zah, oo-nah kah-**meh**-rah
a single room	una singola	oo-nah **seen**-goh-lah
a double room	una doppia	oo-nah **doh**-pee-yah
... with a double bed	una matrimoniale	oo-nah mah-tree-moh-nee-**ah**-leh
with air conditioning	con l'aria condizionata	kohn **lah**-ree-yah kohn-dee-zee-oh-**nah**-tah
with a terrace	con terrazza	kohn ter-**rah**-tsah
with a private bathroom	con il bagno privato	kohn eel bah-nyoh pree-**vah**-toh

Attenzione!

Whenever you fill out a form in Italian, keep in mind that dates are written day/month/year. For example, 9-10-04 (9 *ottobre* 2004) would be October 9, 2004.

In-Room Amenities

Did you forget your hairdryer? Lose your key? No problem.

English	Italian	Pronunciation
I need ...	Mi serve ...	mee ser-veh
alarm clock	la sveglia	lah sveh-lyah
ashtray	il portacenere	eel por-tah-**cheh**-neh-reh

English	Italian	Pronunciation
bathtub	la vasca da bagno	lah vah-skah dah bahn-yoh
blanket	la coperta	lah koh-**per**-tah
blow-dryer	l'asciugacapelli	lah-shoo-gah-kah-**pel**-lee
CD	il CD	eel chee dee
DVD	il DVD	eel dee vee dee
elevator	l'ascensore	lah-shen-**soh**-reh
fax	il fax	eel fax
heat	il riscaldamento	eel ree-skahl-dah-**men**-toh
ice	il ghiaccio	eel ghee-**ah**-choh
Internet	internet	in-ter-net
key	la chiave	lah kee-**yah**-veh
pillow	il cuscino	eel koo-**shee**-noh
remote control	il telecomando	eel teh-leh-koh-**man**-doh
refrigerator	il frigorifero	eel free-goh-**ree**-feh-roh
safe (deposit box)	la cassaforte	lah kahs-sah-**for**-teh
shower	la doccia	lah doh-chah
soap	il sapone	eel sah-**poh**-neh
stairway	la scala, la scalinata	lah skah-lah, lah skah-**lee**-nah-tah
telephone	il telefono	eel teh-**leh**-foh-noh
television	la televisione	lah teh-leh-vee-zee-**oh**-neh
toilet paper	la carta igienica	lah kar-tah ee-**jen**-ee-kah
towel	l'asciugamano	lah-shoo-gah-**mah**-noh
transformer	il trasformatore	eel trah-sfor-mah-**toh**-reh

When in Roma ...

If you're traveling in pairs, it's always better to clearly indicate what kind of bed you require. Do you prefer *un letto matrimoniale* (generally a Queen-size bed) or *due singole* (two singles)? You may require *un lettino in più* (an extra cot) for children.

Problems and Complaints

The squeaky wheel gets the oil. If your accommodations are not quite what you had hoped for, ask for something different. It can't hurt.

English	Italian	Pronunciation
This room is too ...	Questa stanza è troppo ...	kwes-tah stan-zah ay trohp-poh
... small.	... piccola.	**pee**-koh-lah
... dark.	... buia.	boo-yah
... noisy.	... rumorosa.	roo-moh-**roh**-zah
I can't sleep.	Non posso dormire.	nohn pos-soh dor-**mee**-reh
There's no hot water.	Non c'è l'acqua calda.	nohn chay lah-kwah kal-dah
The air conditioner doesn't work.	Non funziona l'aria condizionata.	nohn foon-tsee-**oh**-nah **lah**-ree-yah kohn-dee-zee-oh-**nah**-tah
The toilet is clogged.	La toilette è bloccata.	lah toy-let ay blohk-**kah**-tah
The bathroom is dirty.	Il bagno è sporco.	eel bah-nyoh ay spor-koh

English	Italian	Pronunciation
The sheets are soiled.	Le lenzuola sono sporche.	leh len-**zwoh**-leh soh-noh spor-keh
There's a bad smell in the room.	C'è un'odore cattivo nella camera.	chay oon-oh-**doh**-reh kaht-**tee**-voh nel-lah kah-meh-rah
There's a monster under the bed.	C'è un mostro sotto il letto.	chay oon moh-stroh soht-toh eel leht-toh

When in Roma ...

La mancia (tip) is always appreciated by those who take pride in their work, and most housekeepers deserve it! Five or ten euro can go a long way, and your gesture will be appreciated.

Other Useful Phrases at the Hotel

Should the concierge not speak English, you'll be glad you bought this book. Some useful expressions you may require at the hotel are included here.

English	Italian	Pronunciation
I'd like to make a reservation.	Vorrei fare una prenotazione.	voh-**reh** fah-reh oo-nah preh-noh-tah-tsee-**oh**-neh
... for one person	... per una persona	per oo-nah per-**soh**-nah
... for two/four people	... per due/quattro persone	per doo-eh/kwah-troh per-**soh**-neh

continues

continued

English	Italian	Pronunciation
How much does it cost per day?	Quanto costa al giorno?	kwahn-toh koh-stah ahl jor-noh
Isn't there anything less expensive?	Non c'è qualcosa più economico?	nohn chay kwahl-**koh**-zah pyoo eh-koh-**noh**-mee-koh
Is there a senior citizen discount?	C'è lo sconto per i pensionati?	chay loh skon-toh per ee pen-see-oh-**nah**-tee
Is there a student discount?	C'è lo sconto per gli studenti?	chay lo skon-toh per ylee stoo-**den**-tee
I'd like to pay with ...	Vorrei pagare ...	vohr-**reh** pah-gah-reh
... cash.	... in contanti.	een kohn-**tan**-tee
... check.	... con assegno.	kohn ahs-**sen**-yoh
... credit card.	... con carta di credito.	kohn kar-tah dee **kreh**-dee-toh
Can you please wake me at 7?	Mi può svegliare alle sette per favore?	mee pwoh sveh-**lyah**-reh ahl-leh seht-teh per fah-**voh**-reh
Is breakfast included?	La colazione è compresa?	ay koh-lah-tsee-**oh**-neh **ay** kom-**preh**-zah
At what time is check-out?	Qual è l'ora di partenza?	kwah-**lay** loh-rah dee par-**ten**-zah
Did I receive any messages?	Ho ricevuto dei messaggi?	oh ree-cheh-**voo**-toh dey mes-**sah**-jee
May I leave a message?	Posso lasciare un messaggio?	pohs-soh lah-**shah**-reh oon mes-**sah**-joh
Will you come to bed with me?	Vieni a letto con me?	vee-**yeh**-nee ah let-toh kohn meh

La Bella Lingua

In Italian, the word for floor is *piano* (just like the instrument). The *primo piano* (first floor) is actually the floor above the *pianterreno* (ground floor) and equal to what is considered the second floor in the United States. By the way, the number 13 is considered *buona fortuna*—just the opposite from what one might expect. But watch out for 17 ....

Chapter 7

Eat Your Way to Fluency

In This Chapter

- Grocery markets and specialty shops
- Names of food and beverages
- Simple grocery requests
- Table talk
- At the *ristorante*
- Mini-menu guide

Food seems to be *una lingua internazionale* that everyone speaks. Italians understand, however, that nourishment is only one aspect of food. In addition to eating, the table is a place to connect with *amici* and *famiglia*, and to realign and relax.

Food Stores

First things first—stock up on goodies. You'll find exactly what you crave, as long as you know where to look! (Except, perhaps, peanut butter.)

Store	Negozio	Store	Negozio
bakery	la panetteria	ice cream shop	la gelateria
bar	il bar	market	il mercato
butcher	la macelleria	pastry shop	la pasticceria
dairy store	la latteria	supermarket	il supermercato
fish store	la pescheria	wine bar	l'enoteca
grocery store	l'alimentare	wine store	l'enoteca

Fruits and Vegetables

Visiting the local *mercato* is a feast for the eyes as well as *la bocca* (the mouth). You'll find all the fruits, vegetables, and spices you could ever hope for in the following list.

English	Italian	English	Italian
almond	la mandorla	lettuce	la lattuga
anise	l'anice	melon	il melone
apple	la mela	mint	la menta
apricot	l'albicocca	mushrooms	i funghi
artichoke	il carciofo	mustard	la senape
asparagus	gli asparagi	nutmeg	la noce moscata
banana	la banana	olive	l'oliva
basil	il basilico	onion	la cipolla
bay leaf	la foglia di alloro	orange	l'arancia
beans	i fagioli	oregano	l'origano
cabbage	il cavolo	paprika	la paprika
caper	il cappero	parsley	il prezzemolo
carrots	le carote	peach	la pesca
cauliflower	il cavolfiore	pear	la pera

English	Italian	English	Italian
cherries	le ciliegie	peas	i piselli
chestnut	la castagna	pepper	il pepe
chives	le cipolline	persimmon	il caco
corn	il mais	pineapple	l'ananas
date	il dattero	pistachio nut	il pistacchio
dill	l'aneto	pomegranate	la melagrana
eggplant	la melanzana	potato	le patate
figs	i fichi	raisin	l'uva secca
fruit	la frutta	rice	il riso
garlic	l'aglio	rosemary	il rosmarino
ginger	lo zenzero	saffron	lo zafferano
grapefruit	il pompelmo	salt	il sale
grapes	l'uva	spinach	gli spinaci
green beans	i fagiolini	sugar	lo zucchero
hazelnut	la nocciola	tomatoes	i pomodori
honey	il miele	vegetables	la verdura
legumes	i legumi	walnut	la noce
lemon	il limone	zucchini	gli zucchini

Meat and Dairy

The root of the word *carnevale* (carnival) is *carne* (meat). Meats and poultry are best when selected by your local *macellaio* (butcher). You'll find *formaggio* (cheese) and *il latte* (milk) at *la latteria* (the dairy store).

English	Italian	English	Italian
beef	il manzo	meat	la carne
butter	il burro	milk	il latte

continues

continued

English	Italian	English	Italian
cheese	il formaggio	pork	il maiale
chicken	il pollo	pork chop	la braciola
cold cuts	i salumi	quail	la quaglia
cream	la panna	rabbit	il coniglio
cutlet	la costoletta	salami	il salame
duck	l'anatra	sausage	la salsiccia
eggs	le uova	steak	la bistecca
fillet	il filetto	turkey	il tacchino
ham	il prosciutto	veal	il vitello
lamb	l'agnello	yogurt	lo yogurt
liver	il fegato		

La Pescheria (The Fish Store)

Ahh, *i frutti di mare!* Go to any seaside village in Italy and you're guaranteed to eat some of the best seafood you've ever had.

English	Italian	English	Italian
anchovies	le acciughe	salmon	il salmone
cod	il merluzzo	sardines	le sardine
crab	il granchio	scallops	le cappe sante
fish	il pesce	shrimp	i gamberetti
flounder	la passera	sole	la sogliola
halibut	l'halibut	squid	i calamari
herring	l'aringa	swordfish	la pesce spada
lobster	l'aragosta	trout	la trota
mussel	la cozza	tuna	il tonno
oyster	l'ostrica	whities	i bianchetti

La Dolce Vita

I dolci (sweets) are always a delight, whatever your age. Sweeten up things with some of the following:

The Candy	La Caramella
candy	la caramella
chocolate	la cioccolata
cough drop	una caramella per la tosse
gum	la gomma americana
licorice	la liquirizia
mint	la menta
sugar	lo zucchero

Quench Your Thirst

How about *un bicchiere di vino rosso* (a glass of red wine)? Not your style? Then try a nice cool glass of *acqua minerale con gas* (sparkling mineral water).

When in Roma ...

As is the Italian way, certain times befit certain beverages. *Il cappuccino* is generally consumed in the morning with a *cornetto* (similar to a croissant). *L'espresso* can be consumed any time of the day but is usually taken after meals (never *cappuccino*).

Drinks	Le Bibite
beer	la birra
coffee	il caffè
decaffeinated coffee	il caffè decaffeinato
freshly squeezed juice	la spremuta
fruit juice	il succo di frutta
hot chocolate	la cioccolata calda
iced tea	il tè freddo
lemon soda	la limonata
milk	il latte
mineral water	l'acqua minerale
sparkling mineral water	l'acqua minerale gassata/ frizzante
non-carbonated mineral water	l'acqua minerale naturale
orange soda	l'aranciata
sparkling wine	lo spumante
tea	il tè
wine	il vino

What's What

If you want a freshly squeezed juice, ask for a *spremuta*. If you want a bottle of juice, ask for *un succo di frutta*.

Fine Wine

Italian wines fulfill one fifth of the total world production. Finer wines are classified on the wine label as *denominazione di origine controllata* (DOC) or *denominazione di origine controllata e garantita* (DOCG).

Wine	Il Vino
house wine	il vino della casa
red wine	il vino rosso
rosè wine	il rosè
white wine	il vino bianco
dry wine	il vino secco
sweet wine	il vino dolce
sparkling wine	lo spumante

You Asked for It: You Got It!

It's easy enough to point your finger at something, even if you don't the Italian name. Here are some useful requests for when you're food shopping.

English	Italian	Pronunciation
I would like	Vorrei	vohr-**reh**
Please give me	Per favore mi dia	per fah-**voh**-reh mee dee-ah
Can you give me	Mi può dare	mee pwoh dah-reh
I'll take ...	Prendo ...	pren-doh
a bag of	un saccetto di	oon sahk-**keht**-toh dee
a bottle of	una bottiglia di	oo-nah boht-**tee**-lyah dee

continues

continued

English	Italian	Pronunciation
a box of	una scatola di	oo-nah **skah**-toh-lah dee
a can of	una lattina di	oo-nah laht-**tee**-nah dee
a dozen	una dozzina di	oo-nah doh-**zee**-nah dee
a kilo of	un chilo di	oon kee-loh dee
a little of	un po' di	oon poh dee
a pack of	un pacchetto di	oon pahk-**keht**-toh dee
a piece of	un pezzo di	oon peh-tsoh dee
a portion of	una porzione di	oo-nah por-zee-**oh**-neh dee
a quarter pound of	un etto di	oon eht-toh dee
a slice of	una fetta di	oo-nah feht-tah dee
this	questo	kweh-stoh
that	quello	kwehl-loh

At the *Ristorante*

Eating in different restaurants is a part of the traveler's experience. When you call a restaurant (or after you arrive), you may hear or want to use the following *espressioni*.

English	Italian	Pronunciation
I'd like ….	Vorrei ….	vohr-**reh**
I'd like to make a reservation …	Vorrei fare una prenotazione …	vohr-**reh** fah-reh oo-nah preh-noh-tah-tsee-**oh**-neh
… for 8:00	… alle otto	ahl-leh oht-toh
… for this evening	… per stasera	per stah-**seh**-rah

English	Italian	Pronunciation
… for tomorrow evening	… per domani sera	per doh-**mah**-nee seh-rah
… for two people	… per due persone	per doo-weh per-**soh**-neh
May we sit …	Possiamo sederci …	pohs-see-**yah**-moh seh-**der**-chee
… near the window?	… vicino alla finestra?	vee-**chee**-noh ahl-lah fee-**neh**-strah
… on the terrace?	… sul terrazzo?	sool ter-**rah**-tsoh
How long is the wait?	Quanto tempo si deve aspettare?	kwahn-toh tem-poh see deh-veh ah-spet-**tah**-reh
Make yourselves comfortable.	Vi accomodate.	vee ahk-koh-moh-**dah**-teh
The check, please.	Il conto, per favore.	eel kon-toh per fah-**voh**-rch
Waiter!	Cameriere!	kah-meh-ree-**yeh**-reh
We ate very well.	Abbiamo mangiato molto bene.	ab-bee-**yah**-moh mahn-**jah**-toh mol-toh beh-neh
What do you recommend?	Che cosa consiglia?	kay koh-zah kohn-**see**-lyah
What is the house special?	Qual'è la specialità della casa?	kwah-**leh** lah speh-chah-lee-**tah** dehl-lah kah-zah

Attenzione!

The order of an Italian meal is as important as the food itself. By the way, *l'insalata* is served after the main course.

l'antipasto	appetizer
il primo piatto	first course
il contorno	side dish
il secondo piatto	second course
il dolce	dessert

Expressing Your Needs

Most restaurants are happy to accommodate their clients' needs. Use the following expressions to make your wishes clear.

English	Italian	Pronunciation
I am on a diet.	Sto in dieta.	stoh een dee-**yeh**-tah
I'm a vegetarian.	Sono vegetariano/a.	soh-noh veh-jeh-tah-ree-**ah**-noh/ah
Do you serve kosher food?	Servite del cibo kasher?	ser-**vee**-teh del chee-boh kah-sher
I can't eat anything made with ...	Non posso mangiare niente che contenga ...	nohn pohs-soh man-**jah**-reh nyen-teh keh kon-**ten**-gah
I can't have any ...	Non posso prendere ...	nohn pohs-soh **pren**-deh-reh
... dairy products.	... latticini.	laht-tee-**chee**-nee
... alcohol.	... alcol.	al-col
... shellfish.	... frutti di mare.	froot-tee dee mah-reh

English	Italian	Pronunciation
I'm looking for a dish ...	Cerco un piatto ...	cher-koh oon pee-**aht**-toh
... high in fiber.	... con molta fibra.	kohn mol-tah fee-brah
... low in cholesterol.	... con poco colesterolo.	kohn poh-koh koh-leh-steh **roh**-loh
... low in fat.	... con pochi grassi.	kohn poh-kee grahs-see
... low in sodium.	... poco salato.	poh-koh sah-**lah**-toh
... without preservatives.*	... senza conservanti.	sen-zah kohn-ser-**vahn**-tee
That's enough.	Basta così.	bah-stah coh-**zee**
That's just right.	Va bene così.	vah beh-neh coh-**zee**
That's too much.	È troppo.	ay trohp-poh

Be sure to use the Italian word conservanti *and not the false cognate* preservativi, *which means "prophylactics"!*

The Way You Like It

Order it the way you like it with these terms. Most *ristoranti* will accommodate special requests.

English	Italian	English	Italian
baked	al forno	marinated	marinato
boiled	bollito	medium	normale
breaded	impanato	poached	in camicia
broiled	alla fiamma	rare	al sangue
fried	fritto	steamed	al vapore
grilled	alla griglia	well-done	ben cotto

Kvetching in Italian

Hopefully you won't need to complain, but in case you do, here are the terms you need to describe the *problema*.

English	Italian	Pronunciation
I can't eat this.	Non posso mangiare questo.	nohn pohs-soh mahn-**jah**-reh kweh-stoh
This is ...	Questo è ...	kweh-stoh ay
burned.	bruciato.	broo-**chah**-toh
dirty.	sporco.	spor-koh
overcooked.	troppo cotto.	trohp-poh koht-toh
spoiled/not right.	andato male.	ahn-**dah**-toh mah-leh
too cold.	troppo freddo.	trohp-poh fred-doh
too rare.	troppo crudo.	trohp-poh kroo-doh
too salty.	troppo salato.	trohp-poh sah-**lah**-toh
too spicy.	troppo piccante.	trohp-poh pee-**kahn**-teh
too sweet.	troppo dolce.	trohp-poh dol-cheh
unacceptable.	inaccettabile.	een-ah-cheh-**tah**-bee-leh
My mother makes it better.	Mia madre lo fa meglio.	mee-ah mah-dreh loh fah meh-lyoh

A Mini-Menu Reader

Italian food is as varied as the landscape. The following is a mini-glossary of dishes you may find on *la lista* (the menu).

I Primi

The first course is usually a pasta, risotto, or soup.
Most Italian restaurants will honor your request for
una mezza porzione (half a portion), even if it's not
listed as an option on the menu.

First Course	Il Primo Piatto
broth	brodo
potato pasta with tomato sauce	gnocchi al sugo di pomodoro
lasagna	lasagna
spaghetti in clam sauce	linguine alle vongole
vegetable soup	minestrone
ear-shaped pasta	orecchiette
pasta with beans	pasta e fagioli
tubes of pasta with tomato, vodka, cream, and hot peppers	penne alla vodka
pumpkin ravioli with ricotta cheese	ravioli di zucca e ricotta
seafood risotto	risotto di mare
spaghetti in meat sauce	spaghetti alla bolognese
spaghetti with bacon, egg, and Parmesan	spaghetti alla carbonara
eggdrop soup	stracciatella
tortellini with prosciutto and peas	tortellini prosciutto e piselli
Tuscan country soup	zuppa di verdura Toscana

I Secondi

The second course generally contains the protein
of the meal. You'll have to choose whether you want
la carne (meat), *il pollo* (chicken), or *il pesce* (fish).

Second Course	Il Secondo Piatto
roast lamb spiced with rosemary	agnello arrosto al rosmarino
duck with holy wine (sherry)	anatra con vin santo
steak	bistecca
squid in tomato sauce	calamari alla marinara
monkfish with artichokes	coda di rospo con carciofi
breaded cutlet	cotoletta alla milanese
veal rolls cooked in wine with mushrooms	involtini di vitello
oxtail or veal shanks with lemon, garlic, and parsley	ossobuco alla Milanese
grilled chicken	pollo alla griglia
meatballs in tomato sauce	polpette al ragù
smoked sausage	salsiccia affumicata

I Contorni e Gli Antipasti

Italian *ristoranti* offer more *contorni* (side dishes) and *antipasti* (literally "before the meal") than I could possibly list here. Feel free to order a *contorno* as an appetizer and vice versa.

Side Dish/Appetizer	Il Contorno/L'Antipasto
fried calamari	calamari fritti
marinated artichoke hearts	cuori di carciofo marinati
beans, anchovies, and garlic	fagioli alla veneziana
baked fennel (literally "in a bag")	finocchi al cartoccio
various cheeses	formaggi vari

Side Dish/Appetizer	Il Contorno/L'Antipasto
sautéed mushrooms, garlic, onion, and parsley	funghi trifolati
tomato and onion salad	insalata di pomodoro e cipolla
green salad	insalata verde
grilled eggplant	melanzane alla griglia
boiled potatoes	patate bollite
prosciutto with melon	prosciutto con melone
skewered grilled shrimp	spiedini di gamberi alla griglia
spinach tossed with garlic	spinaci saltati
fried zucchini	zucchini fritti

Chapter 8

Just Looking: Shopping

In This Chapter

- Exchanging money
- Specialty shops
- Talking fashion
- At the camera/electronics store
- Jewelry
- Flowers

A word of advice: Try not to spend all your money the first time you go shopping. (Believe me, you'll be tempted!)

Exchanging Money: *Il Cambio*

Exchanging money does not have to cost you an arm and a leg. It helps to find an exchange that charges you a flat fee, regardless of the amount you are changing. In addition, check the exchange rates to make sure that you are not being shortchanged.

English	Italian	Pronunciation
What is today's exchange rate?	Qual è il cambio d'oggi?	kwahl-**ay** eel **kahm**-bee-oh dohj-jee
Can you give me small change?	Mi può dare degli spiccioli?	mee pwoh dah-reh deh-ylee **spee**-choh-lee
I'd like to cash a traveler's check.	Vorrei cambiare un traveler's check	vohr-**reh** kahm-bee-**ah**-reh oon traveler's check
Do you know where I can find an ATM?	Sa dove posso trovare un Bancomat?	sah doh-veh pohs-soh troh-**vah**-reh oon **bahn**-koh-mat

Where to Spend Your Money: Stores

Specialty shops are a given in Italy. You'll find experts on everything from *sapone* (soap) to *scarpe* (shoes). Ask *Dov'è ...?* (Where is ...?)

The Store	Il Negozio	The Store	Il Negozio
bookstore	la libreria	leather store	la pelletteria
boutique	la bottega	market	il mercato
clothing store	il negozio d'abbigliamento	newspaper stand	il giornalaio
cosmetics shop	la profumeria	pharmacy	la farmacia
department store	il grande magazzino	shoe store	il negozio di scarpe
florist	il fioraio	stationery store	la cartoleria
furniture store	il negozio d'arredamento	tobacco shop	la tabaccheria

When in Ro

Some shopping

- Most stores w
  chases for you.
  made with a cre
  covered for loss

- The I.V.A. (value-added tax) is a
  sales tax attached to all major
  purchases. Save your receipts—
  non-European travelers can apply
  for I.V.A. refunds when they leave
  the country. Ask your travel agency
  for details. Here's how to say "May
  I have a receipt, please?" in Italian:

  Posso avere la ricevuta, per favore?

Just Browsing: Shopping Talk

Helpful shopping-related questions you may hear
or want to ask are included here. If you hear the
salesperson say *Mi dica*, it literally translates to
"Tell me."

Expression	Espressione	Pronunciation
What size do you wear?	Che taglia porta?	kay tah-lyah por-tah
What size shoe?	Che numero di scarpe ha?	kay **noo**-meh-roh dee skar-peh ha
I wear size	Porto la misura	por-toh lah mee-**zoo**-rah

continues

Expression	Espressione	Pronunciation
I wear shoe size ….	Porto il numero ….	por-toh eel **noo**-meh-roh
I'm just looking.	Sto solo guardando.	stoh soh-loh gwar-**dahn**-doh
Where is the fitting room?	Dov'è il camerino?	doh-**vay** eel kah-meh-**ree**-noh
This is too expensive.	Questo è troppo caro.	kweh-stoh **ay** trohp-poh kah-roh
price	il prezzo	eel preh-tsoh
sale	la svendita/ gli sconti	lah sven-dee-tah/ylee skon-tee
sales clerk	il commesso/ la commessa	eel kohm-**mes**-soh/lah kohm-**mes**-sah
shoe size	il numero di scarpe	eel **noo**-meh-roh dee skar-peh
shop window	la vetrina	lah veh-**tree**-nah
size	la misura/ la taglia	lah mee-**zoo**-rah/lah tah-lyah
size: small, medium, large	la taglia: piccola, media, grande	lah tah-lyah: **peek**-koh-lah, **meh**-dee-ah, gran-deh

La Moda (Fashion)

The Italians' ability to mix style with substance is renowned throughout the world. *La moda* (fashion) is a way of life.

Clothing

Italians sure know how to make the most of their assets. To ask for what you want, say *Cerco* ... (I am looking for ....)

English	Italian	English	Italian
article	l'articolo	pullover	il golf/il maglione
bathing suit	il costume da bagno	raincoat	l'impermeabile
bra	il reggiseno	robe	l'accappatoio
clothing	l'abbigliamento	skirt	la gonna
coat	il cappotto/il giubbotto	suit	il completo
dress	l'abito	sweat suit	la tuta da ginnastica
evening dress	l'abito da sera	sweater	la maglia
jeans	i jeans	t-shirt	la maglietta
jacket	la giacca	undershirt	la canottiera
lining	la fodera	underwear:	gli slip:
pajamas	il pigiama	... panties	... le mutandine
pants	i pantaloni	... briefs	... le mutande

When in Roma ...

Perhaps you went out *ieri sera*, and now your favorite silk shirt has a *macchia* (stain) on it. Then there's that grass smudge on your pants from the picnic you had in the *parco* the other day. Having fun, aren't we? Here's the lingo you'll need to keep your pants on straight.

English	Italiano
There is ...	C'è ...
... a stain.	... una macchia.
... a missing button.	... un bottone che manca.
... a tear.	... uno strappo.

Can you dry clean this for me?
Mi potete lavare a secco questo?

Can you mend/iron/starch this for me?
Mi potete rammendare/stirare/inamidare questo?

When will it be ready?
Quando sarà pronto?

Accessories

By adding *gli accessori* that best complement your wardrobe, you can look like a million bucks without spending a million *euros*.

English	Italian	English	Italian
accessories	gli accessori	purse	la borsa
belt	la cintura	sandals	i sandali
boots	gli stivali	scarf	la sciarpa
cosmetics	i cosmetici	shoes	le scarpe
gloves	i guanti	slippers	le pantofole
handkerchief	il fazzoletto	sneakers	le scarpe da tennis/ginnastica
hat	il cappello	socks	le calze, i calzini
lingerie	la biancheria intima	stockings	le calze
pantyhose	i collant	umbrella	l'ombrello

Most smaller stores will offer a discount if you ask, especially if you are buying more than one item. It never hurts to ask!

Can you give me a little discount, please?

Mi può fare un piccolo sconto, per favore?

Fabrics

Rather than spend a fortune on designer clothing, you might consider buying the fabrics and having a *sarto* (tailor) sew something custom-made to your style and fit.

Fabric	Tessuto
acetate	l'acetato
cashmere	il cachemire
chiffon	lo chiffon
cotton	il cotone

continues

continued

Fabric	Tessuto
flannel	la flanella
gabardine	il gabardine
knit	la maglia
lace	il merletto
	il pizzo
leather	il cuoio
	la pelle
linen	il lino
nylon	il nylon
rayon	il rayon
silk	la seta
taffeta	il taffettà
velvet	il velluto
wool	la lana

Jewelry

Make sure you go to a reputable gioielleria (jewelry store) when making expensive purchases.

English	Italian	English	Italian
amethyst	l'ametista	pearls	le perle
aquamarine	l'acquamarina	pendant	il ciondolo
bracelet	il braccialetto	pewter	il peltro
cameo	il cameo	platinum	il platino
chain	la catena	precious stone	la pietra preziosa
cufflinks	i gemelli	ring	l'anello
diamond	il diamante	engagement ring	l'anello di fidanzamento

English	Italian	English	Italian
earrings	gli orecchini	wedding ring	la fede
enamel	lo smalto	ruby	il rubino
gold	l'oro	sapphire	lo zaffiro
jade	la giada	silver	l'argento
jewelry	i gioielli	topaz	il topazio
mother-of-pearl	la madreperla	turquoise	il turchese
onyx	l'onice		

Electronics and More

Watches, cameras, and video cameras—all require batteries, replacement parts, and occasional repair. Refer to Chapter 11 for computer-related speak.

English	Italian	English	Italian
adapter	l'adattatore	flash	il "flash"
battery	la batteria, la pila	lens	l'obiettivo
camera	la macchina fotografica	transformer	il trasformatore
clasp	il gancio	videocassette	la videocassetta
exposure	l'esposizione	video recorder	il video-registratore
film	la pellicola, il film	watch	l'orologio
filter	il filtro	watch band	il cinturino

Although life's bigger problems cannot always be resolved with a replacement part, minor victories can be had if you know the right questions. Here are a few to use at the electronics/camera store.

English	Italian	Pronunciation
Can you fix this?	Mi può aggiustare/ riparare questo?	mee pwoh ahj-joo-**stah**-reh/ree-pah-**rah**-reh kweh-stoh
When will it be ready?	Quando sarà pronto?	kwahn-doh sah-**rah** pron-toh
My watch needs a new battery.	Il mio orologio ha bisogno di una batteria nuova.	eel mee-oh oh-roh-**loh**-joh ah bee-**zoh**-nyoh dee oo-nah baht-teh-**ree**-ah nwoh-vah
My camera isn't working.	La mia macchina fotografica non funziona.	lah mee-ah **mahk**-kee-nah foh-toh-**grah**-fee-kah nohn foon-zee-**oh**-nah
I need film.	Ho bisogno della pellicola/di un rullino.	oh bee-**zoh**-nyoh dehl-lah pehl-**lee**-koh-lah/dee oon rool-**lee**-noh
Do you have batteries?	Avete delle batterie?	ah-**veh**-teh dehl-leh baht-teh-**ree**-yeh
I want to have this film developed.	Voglio sviluppare questa pellicola.	voh-lyoh svee-loop-**pah**-reh kwes-tah pehl-**lee**-koh-lah
Please make a copy of this photograph/roll.	Per favore mi faccia una copia di questa/o foto/ rullino?	per fah-**voh**-reh mee fah-chah oo-nah **koh**-pee-ah dee kweh-stah/oh foh-toh/rool-**lee**-noh

La Cartoleria (Stationery Store)

In addition to office supplies, stationery, candy, and cigarettes, *la cartoleria* often sells stamps and bus tickets. It's also a good place to find inexpensive gift items.

Stationery	La Cartoleria	Stationery	La Cartoleria
candy	le caramelle	matches	i fiammiferi
cigarettes	le sigarette	notebook	il quaderno
cigars	i sigari	paper	la carta
gift	il regalo	pen	la penna
a guide-book	una guida	pencil	la matita
lighter	l'accendino	postcard	la cartolina
map	la pianta, la cartina, la mappa	stamp	il francobollo
toys	i giocattoli		

The Florist

Flowers are often associated with particular occasions or with certain emotions. For example, everyone knows that red roses are traditionally used to make a declaration of love, but were you aware that chrysanthemums are given at funerals?

Flower	Il Fiore	Flower	Il Fiore
carnation	il garofano	orchid	l'orchidea
chrysan-themum	il crisantemo	pansy	la viola del pensiero

continues

continued

Flower	Il Fiore	Flower	Il Fiore
daffodil	la giunchiglia	poppy	il papavero
daisy	la margherita	rose	la rosa
dandelion	il dente di leone	sunflower	il girasole
lily	il giglio	violet	la violetta

Chapter 9

Ciao Baby! Flirting and Romance

In This Chapter

- Flirting in Italian
- Making a date
- One-liners
- Intimate questions
- Apologies and excuses

If there's one thing the Italians know, it's *l'amore*. This chapter deals with relationships and gives you the language you need to make a date.

Love and Consequences

Ladies, look out for shoe salesmen! They're in the best position to wow you with their humble expressions of love, and at your feet to boot. Men, watch out for those Italian beauties … they'll steal your heart and throw away the key!

English	Italian	Pronunciation
a date	un appuntamento	oon ahp-poon-tah-**men**-toh
affair	una storia	oo-nah stoh-**ree**-ah
anniversary	l'anniversario	lahn-nee-ver-**sah**-ree-oh
birth control	il controllo delle nascite	eel kohn-**trohl**-loh dehl-leh **nah**-shee-teh
boyfriend	il fidanzato*	eel fee-dan-**zah**-toh
	il ragazzo	eel rah-**gah**-tsoh
celebration	la celebrazione	lah cheh-leh-brah-zee-**oh**-neh
engagement	il fidanzamento	eel fee-dahn-zah-**men**-toh
flowers	i fiori	ee fyoh-ree
friend	l'amico (m.)	lah-**mee**-koh
	l'amica (f.)	lah-**mee**-kah
friendship	l'amicizia	lah-mee-chee-**zee**-ah
girlfriend	la fidanzata*	lah fee-dan-**zah**-tah
	la ragazza	lah rah-**gah**-tsah
hug	l'abbraccio	lah-**brah**-choh
honeymoon	la luna di miele	lah loo-nah dee myeh-leh
husband	il marito/lo sposo	eel mah-**ree**-toh/loh spoh-soh
kiss	il bacio	eel bah-choh
love	l'amore	lah-moh-reh
lover	l'amante	lah-mahn-teh
marriage	il matrimonio	eel mah-tree-**moh**-nee-oh
nuptials	le nozze	leh noh-steh
one-night stand	una storia di una notte	oo-nah stoh-**ree**-ah dee oo-nah noht-teh
relationship	un rapporto	oon rahp-**por**-toh
	una relazione	oo-nah reh-lah-zee-**oh**-neh

English	Italian	Pronunciation
romance	il romanzo	eel roh-**man**-zoh
sex	il sesso	eel ses-soh
Valentine's Day	il giorno di San Valentino	eel jor-noh dee san vah-len-**tee**-noh
wife	la moglie/la sposa	lah moh-lyeh/lah spoh-zah

*fidanzato/fidanzata: *used interchangeably as boyfriend/ girlfriend, fiancé/fiancée*

Useful verbs include the following.

English	Italian	Pronunciation
to caress	accarezzare	ahk-kah-reh-**tsah**-reh
to court	corteggiare	kor-tehj-**jah**-reh
to flirt	flirtare	fleer-**tah**-reh
to make a date	fissare un appuntamento	fees-**sah**-reh oon ahp-poon-tah-**men**-toh
to make love	fare l'amore	fah-reh lah-moh-reh

A Lover's Menu

A candlelit *ristorante*, a bottle of *vino*, homemade pasta, the scent of wisteria, plus a few well-articulated thoughts, and *magica!* Words allow us to express the realm that lives within our minds and hearts. Share yours. All expressions are given in the "tu" (informal) form of the verb.

English	Italian	Pronunciation
Are you married?	Sei sposato/a?	say spoh-**zah**-toh/ah
Can I have your phone number?	Posso avere il tuo numero di telefono?	pohs-soh ah-**veh**-reh eel too-oh **noo**-meh-roh dee teh-**leh**-foh-noh
Can I kiss you?	Posso baciarti?	pohs-soh bah-**char**-tee
Can we meet again?	Possiamo vederci ancora?	pohs-see-**ah**-moh veh-**der**-chee ahn-**koh**-rah
Do you want to come home with me?	Vorresti venire a casa con me?	vor-**reh**-stee veh-**nee**-reh ah kah-zah kohn meh
Haven't we met before?	Non ci siamo già conosciuti un'altra volta?	nohn chee see-**ah**-moh jah koh-noh-**shoo**-tee oon ahl-trah vol-tah
Hey gorgeous!	Ciao bellissima! (f.)	chow bel-**lees**-see-mah
I care for you.	Ti voglio bene.	tee voh-lyoh beh-neh
I don't have a boyfriend/girlfrend.	Non ho un fidanzato/a.	nohn oh oon fee-**dahn**-zah-toh/ah
I love you.	Ti amo.	tee ah-moh
I'm lonely.	Mi sento solo/a.	mee sen-toh soh-loh/ah
Stay with me.	Sta con me.	stah kohn meh
What about dinner tonight?	Vuoi andare a cena stasera?	vwoy ahn-**dah**-reh ah cheh-nah stah-**seh**-rah
What are you doing tomorrow night?	Che fai domani sera?	kay fy doh-**mah**-nee seh-rah
What is your astrological sign?	Di che segno sei?	dee kay seh-nyoh say
What is your name?	Come ti chiami?*	koh-meh tee kee-**ah**-mee
What should we do?	Che cosa facciamo?	kay koh-zah fah-**chah**-moh

English	Italian	Pronunciation
What's a nice girl/guy doing in a place like this?	Cosa ci fa una ragazza/ragazzo come te in questo locale?	koh-zah chee fah oo-nah rah-**gah**-tsah/rah-**gah**-tsoh koh-meh teh een kwel-stoh loh-**kah**-leh
When?	Quando?	kwahn-doh
Why don't we meet at ...	Perché non ci incontriamo a ...	per-**kay** nohn chee een-kohn-tree-**ah**-moh ah
Do you want to marry me?	Mi vuoi sposare?	mee vwoy spoh-**zah**-reh
Would you like to go out?	Vorresti uscire?	vohr-**reh**-stee oo-**shee**-reh
You are beautiful.	Sei bellissimo/a.	say behl-**lees**-see-moh/ah
You are fascinating.	Sei affascinante.	say ahf-fah-shee-**nahn**-teh
Your place or mine?	Casa tua o casa mia?	kah-zah too-ah oh kah-zah mee-ah

*Informal

What's What

There are two expressions used to indicate "I love you."

Ti amo	Used almost exclusively between intimates and close family members.
Ti voglio bene	Used between intimates, friends, or anyone dear. It literally translates to "I want you well."

In the Bedroom

The Italian language has far more salacious expressions than I feel is appropriate to offer here. You'll have to learn them in person. For now, here's a bedroom primer to help you get started.

English	Italian	Pronunciation
Faster.	Più veloce.	pyoo veh-**loh**-cheh
I like you.	Mi piaci.	mee pee-**ah**-chee
I'm coming!	Vengo!/ Sto venendo!	ven-goh/stoh veh-**nen**-doh
Kiss me.	Baciami.	**bah**-chah-mee
Let's go to bed.	Andiamo a letto.	ahn-dee-**ah**-moh ah leht-toh
Not before dinner.	Non prima di cena.	nohn pree-mah dee cheh-nah
Slower.	Più piano/ lentamente	pyoo pyah-noh/ len-tah-**men**-teh
Touch me.	Toccami.	**tohk**-kah-mee
What did you say your name was again?	Come hai detto che ti chiami?	koh-meh ay deht-toh kay tee kee-**ah**-mee
You're incredible.	Sei incredibile.	say een-kreh-**dee**-bee-leh
You're trouble.	Sei un disastro!	say oon dee-**zah**-stroh
	Porti solo guai!	por-tee soh-loh guai
	Sei un pericolo!	say oon peh-**ree**-koh-loh
You're sweet as honey!	Sei dolce come il miele!	say dohl-cheh koh-meh eel myeh-leh
Do you have condoms?	Hai dei preservativi?*	ay dey preh-zer-vah-**tee**-vee

* *A false cognate, it does not translate to mean "preservatives." Another word for condoms incudes* i profilattici.

La Bella Lingua

Mammone is the term used to describe an unmarried, adult male living at home and highly dependent on his *mamma*. No equivalent word seems to exist for adult females.

Excuses and Apologies

Half the time we spend talking ourselves into trouble, the other half we're trying to find a way out! I make no judgments. Sometimes a simple apology will do the trick. Other times may require a little more imagination.

English	Italian	Pronounciation
I'm sorry.	Mi dispiace.	mee dee-spee-**ah**-chay
I tried calling.	Ho provato a telefonare.	oh proh-**vah**-toh ah teh-leh-foh-**nah**-reh
I lost your number.	Ho perso il tuo numero di telefono.	oh per-soh eel too-oh **noo**-meh-roh dee teh-**leh**-foh-noh
This isn't what it looks like.	Questo non è quello che sembra.	kweh-stoh nohn ay kwehl-loh kay sem-brah
I meant to call.	Avevo l'intenzione di telefonare.	ah-**veh**-voh leen-ten-zee-**oh**-neh dee teh-leh-foh-**nah**-reh
I've been busy.	Sono stato/a molto impegnato/a.	soh-noh stah-toh/ah mohl-toh eem-peh-**nyah**-toh/ah

continues

continued

English	Italian	Pronounciation
I've been away.	Sono stato/a via.	soh-noh stah-toh/ah vee-ah
Please forgive me.	Perdonami.	per-**doh**-nah-mee
I had a bad hair day.	Ho stata una brutta giornata.	oh stah-tah oo-nah broot-tah jor-**nah**-tah
It's that time.	È l'ora.	ay loh-rah
	È il momento giusto.	ay eel moh-**men**-toh joo-stoh
I have a headache.	Ho mal di testa.	oh mahl dee teh-stah

10

Godere di Buona Salute! Staying Healthy

In This Chapter

- At the *dottore*
- At the *dentista*
- At the *farmacia*
- At the *la parrucchiera* (hairdresser) or *il barbiere*
- At the *ottico* (optician)

Like a car's engine, your body requires regular maintenance. This chapter gives you the language you'll need to stay healthy and how to describe when you're not feeling your regular self.

A Collection of Parts: Your Body

Can you see how the Italian word *braccia* (arm) is connected to the word *braccialetto* (bracelet)? And what about those "gams" as legs were once called in Spencer Tracey's day, coming from the Italian word *gambe?* How many *piedi* (feet) are there in a centipede, anyway? Irregular plural forms are provided (in parentheses).

The Body	Il Corpo	Pronunciation
ankle	la caviglia	la kah-**vee**-lyah
appendix	l'appendice	lahp-pen-**dee**-cheh
arm	il braccio (le braccia)	eel brah-choh (leh brah-chah)
back	la schiena	lah skee-**eh**-nah
blood	il sangue	eel sahn-gweh
body	il corpo	eel kor-poh
bone	l'osso (le ossa)	lohs-soh (leh ohs-sah)
brain	il cervello	eel cher-**vehl**-loh
breast	il seno	eel seh-noh
buttock	il sedere	eel seh-**deh**-reh
chest	il petto	eel peht-toh
chin	il mento	eel men-toh
ear	l'orecchio	loh-**rek**-kee-oh
eye	l'occhio	**loh**-kee-oh
face	il viso, la faccia	eel vee-soh, lah fah-chah
finger	il dito (le dita)	eel dee-toh (leh dee-tah)
foot	il piede	eel pee-**eh**-deh
gland	la ghiandola	lah ghee-**ahn**-doh-lah
hand	la mano (le mani)	lah mah-noh (leh mah-nee)
head	la testa	lah teh-stah
heart	il cuore	eel kwoh-reh
joint	l'articolazione	lar-tee-koh-lah-zee-**oh**-neh
knee	il ginocchio (le ginocchia)	eel jee-**nohk**-kee-oh (leh jee-**nohk**-kee-ah)
leg	la gamba	lah gahm-bah
ligament	il legamento	eel leh-gah-**men**-toh

The Body	Il Corpo	Pronunciation
mouth	la bocca	lah bohk-kah
muscle	il muscolo	eel **moo**-skoh-loh
nails	le unghie	leh oon-gyeh
neck	il collo	eel kohl-loh
nose	il naso	eel nah-zoh
skin	la pelle	lah pehl-leh
shoulder	la spalla	lah spahl-lah
stomach	lo stomaco	loh **stoh**-mah-koh
throat	la gola	lah goh-lah
toe	il dito	eel dee-toh
tongue	la lingua	lah leen-gwah
tooth	il dente	eel den-teh
wrist	il polso	eel pol-soh

What Ails You?

The doctor or pharmacist may ask you a few questions, some of which are included here:

What is the problem?	Qual è il problema?
How do you feel?	Come si sente?* (formal)
How old are you?	Quanti anni ha?
How long have you been suffering?	Da quanto tempo soffre?
Are you taking any medications?	Prende delle medicine?
Do you have any allergies?	Ha delle allergie?
Do you suffer from …?	Soffre di …?
Have you had …?	Ha avuto …?
What hurts you?	Che cosa Le fa male?

*Come ti senti? *(informal)*

Tell Me Where It Hurts

The following expressions will help you describe your discomfort or pain. Substitute the appropriate body part, offered in parentheses, using the terms in the preceding section.

English	Italian	Pronunciation
I feel bad.	Mi sento male.	mee sen-toh mah-leh
I don't feel well.	Non mi sento bene.	nohn mee sen-toh beh-neh
I am exhausted.	Sono esausto/a.	soh-noh eh-**zow**-stoh/ah
It hurts here.	Mi fa male qui.	mee fah mah-leh kwee
My (head) hurts.	Mi fa male (la testa).*	mee fah mah-leh (lah teh-stah)
I have/I suffer from ...	Ho/Soffro di ...	oh/sohf-froh dee
... a bad heart.	... mal di cuore.	mahl dee kwoh-reh
... a cough.	... la tosse.	lah tohs-seh
... a fever.	... la febbre.	lah feb-breh
... a stomachache.	... mal di stomaco.	mahl dee stoh-**mah**-koh
... nausea.	... la nausea.	lah **now**-zee-ah
... sore throat.	... mal di gola.	mahl dee goh-lah

You may replace the word in parentheses with another to describe your specific problem.

Aches and Pains

Bad things happen to good people. Discomfort is a fact of life, especially when you're in transit. Get specific with these terms, all offered with the appropriate article.

Symptom	Il Sintomo	Pronunciation
abscess	un ascesso	oon ah-**shehs**-soh
blister	la vescica	lah veh-**shee**-kah
blood	il sangue	eel sahn-gweh
broken bone	un osso rotto	oon ohs-soh roht-toh
bruise	un livido	oon **lee**-vee-doh
bump	una botta	oo-nah boht-tah
burn	una scottatura	oo-nah skoht-tah-**too**-rah
chills	i brividi	ee **bree**-vee-dee
constipation	la stitichezza	lah stee-tee-**keh**-tsah
cough	la tosse	lah tohs-seh
cramps	i crampi	ee kram-pee
diarrhea	la diarrea	lah dee-ahr-**reh**-ah
dizziness	le vertigini	leh ver-**tee**-jee-nee
exhaustion	l'esaurimento	leh-zow-ree-**men**-toh
fever	la febbre	lah feb-breh
fracture	una frattura	oo-nah frat-**too**-rah
headache	il mal di testa	eel mahl dee teh-stah
indigestion	l'indigestione	leen-dee-jes-tee-**oh**-neh
insomnia	l'insonnia	leen-**sohn**-nee-ah
lump (on the head)	un bernoccolo	oon ber-**nohk**-koh-loh
migraine	l'emicrania	leh-mee-**krah**-nee-ah
nausea	la nausea	lah now-**zee**-ah
pain	un dolore	oon doh-**loh**-reh
rash	un'irritazione	oon-eer-ree-tah-zee-**oh**-neh
sprain	una distorsione	oo-nah dee-stor-see-**oh**-neh
stomachache	il mal di stomaco	eel mahl dee **stoh**-mah-koh
swelling	un gonfiore	oon gohn-**fyoh**-reh
toothache	un mal di denti	oon mahl dee den-tee
wound	una ferita	oo-nah feh-**ree**-tah

Diseases

The word *disease* literally means "not at ease." Should you have to visit the doctor, he or she is going to ask you to fill out a form, tell about any medications you're taking, and answer questions about preexisting medical conditions.

Illness	La Malattia	Illness	La Malattia
AIDS	l'AIDS	gout	la gotta
angina	l'angina	heart attack	l'infarto
appendicitis	l'appendicite	hemophilia	l'emofilia
asthma	l'asma	hepatitis	l'epatite
bronchitis	la bronchite	measles	il morbillo
cancer	il cancro	mumps	gli orecchioni
cold	il raffreddore	pneumonia	la polmonite
diabetes	il diabete	polio	la poliomielite
drug addiction	la tossico-dipendenza	stroke	il colpo apoplettico
dysentery	la dissenteria	sunstroke	il colpo di sole
flu	l'influenza	tetanus	il tetano
German measles	la rosolia	tuberculosis	la tubercolosi
gonorrhea	lah gonorrea	whooping cough	la pertosse

Medical Emergencies

In an *emergenzia*, you don't need to worry about anything more than getting your point across quickly and clearly. Start with *Aiuto!* (Help!)

English	Italian	Pronunciation
Help!	Aiuto!	ay-**yoo**-toh
Call ...	Chiamate	kee-ah-**mah**-teh
... an ambulance!	... un'ambulanza!	oon-ahm-boo-**lahn**-zah
... the emergency medical service!	... il pronto soccorso!	eel pron-toh sohk-**kor**-soh
... a doctor!	... un medico!	oon **meh**-dee-koh
I am allergic to	Sono allergico/a a	soh-noh ahl-**ler**-jee-koh/ah ah
I can't breathe.	Non posso respirare.	nohn pohs-soh reh-spee-**rah**-reh
I have a wound.	Ho una ferita.	oh oo-nah feh-**ree**-tah
I'm diabetic.	Sono diabetico/a.	soh-noh dee-ah-**beh**-tee-koh/ah
It hurts.	Fa male.	fah mah-leh
There's a lot of blood.	C'è molto sangue.	chay mohl-toh sahn-gweh
Where is the hospital?	Dov'è l'ospedale?	doh-vay loh-speh-**dah**-leh

Alla Farmacia (At the Pharmacy)

Your doctor may give you a *ricetta medica* (prescription) to be filled at the *farmacia* or *drogheria*. The following sentences all express possible questions you may have for the *farmacista*.

English	Italian	Pronunciation
Do you have anything for ...?	Avete qualcosa per ...?	ah-veh-teh kwahl-**koh**-zah per

continues

continued

English	Italian	Pronunciation
Do you know where I can find an (all-night) pharmacy?	Sa dove posso trovare una farmacia (notturna)?	sah doh-veh pohs-soh troh-**vah**-reh oo-nah far-mah-**chee**-ah noht-**toor**-nah
I need	Ho bisogno di	oh bee-**zoh**-nyoh dee
Is a prescription necessary?	Mi serve una ricetta medica?	mee ser-veh oo-nah ree-**chet**-tah **meh**-dee-kah

Before you even visit a doctor, you might want to try the pharmacist. The *farmacista* can often provide you with something for immediate relief.

English	Italian	English	Italian
ace bandage	la fascia elastica	mirror	lo specchio
antibiotics	gli antibiotici	mud	il fango
antiseptic	l'antisettico	nail file	la limetta
aspirin	l'aspirina	nail polish	lo smalto per le unghie
baby bottle	il biberon	needle and thread	l'ago ed il filo
bandages	i cerotti	nose drops	le gocce per il naso
body lotion	la crema per il corpo	pacifier	il ciuccio
brush	la spazzola	pills	le pastiglie
castor oil	l'olio di ricino	prescription	la ricetta medica
comb	il pettine	razor	il rasoio
conditioner	il balsamo	safety pin	la spilla di sicurezza

English	Italian	English	Italian
condoms	i preservativi*	sanitary napkins	gli assorbenti
contraception	la contraccezione	scissors	le forbici
cotton balls	i batuffoli di cotone	shampoo	lo shampoo
cotton swabs**	i cottonfioc	shaving cream	la crema da barba
cough syrup	lo sciroppo per la tosse	sleeping pill	il sonnifero
deodorant	il deodorante	soap	il sapone
depilatory wax	la ceretta depilatoria	syringe	la siringa
diapers	i pannolini	talcum powder	il talco
eye drops	il collirio	tampons	i tamponi
floss	il filo interdentale	thermometer	il termometro
gauze bandages	le bende	tissues	i fazzoletti
hairspray	la lacca	toothbrush	lo spazzolino da denti
heating pad	l'impacco caldo	toothpaste	il dentifricio
ice pack	la borsa del ghiaccio	tweezers	le pinzette
laxative	il lassativo	vitamins	le vitamine

Also, i profilattici

**For ears*

Al Dente? At the Dentist

My father always insisted, "Take care of your teeth!" He was right. Keep those choppers in good shape with these terms.

English	Italiano	English	Italiano
braces	Apparecchio correttore	gums	le gengive
bridge	il ponte	jaw	la mascella
cavity	la carie	nerve	il nervo
crown	la corona	tooth	il dente
dentist	il/la dentista (m./f.)	toothache	il mal di denti
denture	la dentiera	widsom tooth	il dente del giudizio

That's *Capelli*, Not *Capellini*: Your Hair

In Italy, women go to *la parrucchiera* (hairdresser). Men visit *il barbiere* (barber, from *barba*, meaning "beard" and the root of the word *barbarian*.)

English	Italiano	Pronunciation
I'd like ...	Vorrei ...	vohr-**reh**
to blow dry my hair.	asciugare i capelli.	ah-shoo-**gah**-reh ee kah-**pehl**-lee
to color my hair.	tingere i capelli.	**teen**-jeh-reh ee kah-**pehl**-lee
to curl my hair.	farmi i riccioli.	far-mee ee **ree**-choh-lee

English	Italiano	Pronunciation
to have my hair cut.	farmi tagliare i capelli.	far-mee tah-**lyah**-reh ee kah-**pehl**-lee
to get a manicure/ pedicure.	farmi fare la manicure/ pedicure.	far-mee fah-reh lah mah-nee-**koo**-reh/ peh-dee-**koo**-reh
to get a permanent.	farmi la permanente.	far-mee lah per-mah-**nen**-teh
to shampoo.	farmi lo shampoo.	far-mee loh sham-poo
a shave.	farmi la barba.	far-mee lah bar-bah
to wax my legs.	farmi la ceretta alle gambe.	far-mee lah cheh-**ret**-tah ahl-leh gahm-beh

When in Roma ...

Shop at *la profumeria* (the cosmetics store) for items related to *il trucco* (literally, "the trick" and meaning "make-up"):

blush	*il fard*
eye shadow	*l'ombretto*
nail polish	*lo smalto per le unghie*
perfume	*il profumo*

Dall'Ottico: **At the Optician's**

It's difficult to go sightseeing if you've lost your glasses. The next time you travel, you might want to bring an extra pair, just in case.

English	Italian	English	Italian
astigmatism	l'astigmatismo	glasses	gli occhiali
contact lens	le lenti a contatto	sunglasses	gli occhiali da sole
eyes	gli occhi	lens	le lenti
far-sighted	presbite	near-sighted	miope
frame	la montatura	prescription	la ricetta medica

Chapter 11

Business and Communications

In This Chapter

- Using the *telefono*
- At the post office
- Talking business and finance
- Learning computer lingo
- The *polizia* and general emergencies

Whether for business or pleasure, a few skills can take you a long way: making *una telefonata*, writing a *lettera*, and being able to read the small print in a business contract or bank statement. I've also included useful computer lingo. Finally, you'll find the language you need in the event of an emergency.

Il Telefono

It's always a good idea to find out any local numbers that you might need in a quandary. Types of calls you may make include the following:

collect call	una telefonata a carico del destinatario
credit card call	una telefonata con carta di credito
long-distance call	una telefonata interurbana
intercontinental call	una telefonata intercontinentale
international call*	una telefonata internazionale
person-to-person call	una telefonata con preavviso
local call	una telefonata urbana

Within Europe

Telephone Talk

It's a good idea to buy yourself *una scheda telefonica* (telephone card) at the airport and keep it with you at all times. Make sure you break off the corner before inserting it into the payphone.

Expression	Espressione	Pronunciation
With whom do I speak?	Con chi parlo?	kohn kee par-loh
I would like to make a phone call.	Vorrei fare una telefonata.	vohr-**reh** fah-reh oo-nah teh-leh-foh-**nah**-tah
Do you sell telephone cards?	Vendete schede telefoniche?	ven-**deh**-teh skeh-deh teh-leh-**foh**-nee-keh
Hello!*	Pronto!	prohn-toh
Is (Robert) there?	C'è (Roberto)?	chay …
It's (Gabriella).	Sono (Gabriella).	soh-noh …
I'd like to speak with ….	Vorrei parlare con ….	vohr-**reh** par-**lah**-reh kohn
I'll call back later.	richiamo più tardi.	ree-kee-**ah**-moh pyoo tar-dee

Used only on the telephone and literally meaning "Ready!"

Attenzione!

In case of emergency, keep these helpful contact numbers handy:

General SOS (free from any telephone): 113

Carabinieri (police; free): 112

Automobile club d'Italia (car accidents and breakdowns): 116

Dealing with the Operator

Maybe you need help getting your point across. The line is busy. You can't connect.

English	Italian	Pronunciation
I have a problem.	Ho un problema.	oh oon proh-**bleh**-mah
The line was disconnected.	È caduta la linea.	ay kah-**doo**-tah lah **lee**-neh-ah
The line is always busy.	La linea è sempre occupata.	lah **lee**-neh-ah ay sem-preh ohk-koo-**pah**-tah
Excuse me, I dialed the wrong number.	Mi scusi, ho sbagliato numero.	mee skoo-zee oh sbah-**lyah**-toh **noo**-meh-roh
I can't get a line.	Non posso prendere la linea.	nohn pohs-soh **pren**-deh-reh lah **lee**-neh-ah
May I speak with an international operator?	Posso parlare con un operatore internazionale?	con pohs-soh par-**lah**-reh kohn oon oh-per-ah-**toh**-reh een-ter-nah-zee-oh-**nah**-leh

continues

continued

English	Italian	Pronunciation
Is there someone that speaks English?	C'è qualcuno che parla l'inglese?	chay kwahl-**koo**-noh kay par-lah leen-**gleh**-zeh

What the operator might say:

What number did you dial?	*Che numero ha fatto?*
No one is answering.	*Non risponde nessuno.*
That number is out of service.	*Quel numero di telefono è fuori servizio.*
Hold.	*Attendere.*

Additional telephone-related terms include the following:

800 number (free)	un numero verde	fax number	il numero di fax
answering machine	la segreteria telefonica	line	la linea
area code	il prefisso	message	il messaggio
telephone booth	la cabina telefonica	operator	l'operatore
cellular phone	il telefonino/ il cellulare	phone card	la scheda telefonica
coin return	la restituzione monete	public phone	il telefono pubblico
fax/fax machine	il facsimile/ il fax	telephone book	l'elenco telefonico
fax modem	il fax modem	Yellow Pages	le pagine gialle
to call back	Richiamare	to make a call	fare una telefonata

to dial	comporre il numero	to receive a call	ricevere una telefonata
to drop a line	dare un colpo di telefono	to ring	suonare/squillare
to hold	attendere	to send a fax	inviare un fax/ "faxare"
to insert the card	introdurre la carta	to speak to an operator	parlare con un operatore
to leave a message	lasciare un messaggio	to telephone	telefonare

At L'Ufficio Postale (Post Office)

Whether you're looking to buy *francobolli* (stamps) or want to send *un pacco* (a package), a word of advice when visiting the *ufficio postale*: *Pazienza* (patience)!

English	Italian	Pronunciation
I'd like to send this …	Vorrei spedire questo …	vohr-**reh** speh-**dee**-reh kweh-stoh
… by airmail.	…per posta aerea.	per poh-stah ah-**eh**-reh-ah
… by express mail.	… per espresso.	per eh-**spres**-soh
… by registered mail.	… per posta raccomandata.	per poh-stah rahk-koh-mahn-**dah**-tah
… by special delivery.	… per corriere speciale.	per kor-ree-**yeh**-reh speh-**chah**-leh
… by C.O.D.	… con pagamento alla consegna.	kohn pah-gah-**men**-toh ahl-lah kohn-**seh**-nyah
When will (it) arrive?	Quando arriverà?	kwahn-doh ahr-ree-veh-**rah**

continues

continued

English	Italian	Pronunciation
How many stamps are required to send this letter to ...?	Quanti francobolli ci vogliono per inviare questa lettera a ...?	kwahn-tee fran-koh-**bohl**-lee chee **voh**-lyoh-noh per een-vee-**ah**-reh kweh-stah **leht**-teh-rah ah
I'd like to insure this package.	Vorrei assicurare questo pacco.	vohr-**reh** ahs-see-koo-**rah**-reh kweh-stoh pahk-koh

Here are some other useful terms for sending and receiving mail:

addressee	il recipiente	post office	l'ufficio postale
cardboard box	la scatola di cartone	post office box	la casella postale
counter/ window	lo sportello	postage	la tariffa postale
envelope	la busta	extra postage	la soprattassa postale
letter	la lettera	postal worker	l'impiegato postale
mail	la posta	postcard	la cartolina
mail carrier	il postino	receipt	la ricevuta
mailbox	la cassetta della posta; la buca	sender	il mittente
money transfer	il vaglia postale, il vaglia telegrafico	stamps	i francobolli
package	il pacco	telegram	il telegramma
packing paper	la carta da pacchi		

La Bella Lingua

You may not be able to write the entire letter in Italian, but a few Italian terms can always spice up any correspondence.

Dear (informal)	*Caro/a*
Dear (formal)	*Egregio/a*
Affectionately	*Affettuosamente*
Cordially (formal)	*Cordialmente*
Yours (informal)	*Il tuo/la tua*
Yours (formal)	*Il Suo/la Sua*
Sincerely (formal)	*Sinceramente*
Until later	*A più tardi*
A hug	*Un abbraccio*
A big kiss	*Un bacione*

The Language of Money

Money makes a lot possible. Finance-related terms are included here.

English	Italian	English	Italian
ATM	Il Bancomat	final payment	il saldo
balance	l'estratto conto	guarantee	la garanzia
bank	la banca	holder	il titolare
bank account	il conto bancario	interest	l'interesse
bill	la bolletta	investment	l'investimento

continues

continued

English	Italian	English	Italian
to borrow	prendere in prestito	loan	il prestito
branch	la filiale	money	i soldi/il denaro
cash	i contanti	monthly statement	l'estratto conto
cashier	il cassiere	mortgage	il mutuo
change	gli spiccioli	payment	il pagamento
exchange	il cambio	rate	la rata
check	l'assegno	receipt	la ricevuta
checkbook	il libretto degli assegni	sale	la vendita
checking account	il conto corrente	savings book	il libretto di risparmio
coins	le monete	signature	la firma
credit	il credito	stock	l'azione
currency	la valuta	sum	la somma
customer	il cliente	teller	l'impiegato di banca
debt	il debito	total	il totale
deposit	il deposito	traveler's check	travel check
down payment	l'anticipo	window	lo sportello
exchange rate	il tasso di scambio		

Il Computer

Many travelers bring along their laptop computers. Learn the lingo with the following terms.

English	Italian	English	Italian
adapter	l'adattatore	printer	la stampante
address	l'indirizzo	screen	lo schermo
at (@)	la chiocciola	search engine	il motore di ricerca
battery	la batteria, la pila	to back up	backuppare
computer	il computer	to burn	masterizzare
dialog box	la finestra di dialogo	to chat online	ciattare
disks	i dischetti	to click	cliccare
e-mail	la posta elettronica	to connect	connettersi
folder	la cartella	to crash	andare in bomba
Internet	la rete; l'internet	to debug	debuggare
keyboard	la tastiera	to download	daunlodare
laptop computer	il computer portatile	to format	formattare
mouse	il mouse	to scan	scandire
online	in linea	to surf the web	surfare/navigare
page	la pagina	to zip	zippare
password	la parola d'accesso/codice	website	il sito internet; il sito

Urgente!

Your purse was stolen. You lost your passport. You need help. In the event of a vehicular emergency, refer back to Chapter 5. Similarly, for health-related situations, refer back to Chapter 11.

English	Italian	Pronunciation
Help!	Aiuto!	ay-**yoo**-toh
Call an ambulance!	Chiamate un'ambulanza!	kee-ah-**mah**-teh oon-am-boo-lan-zah
Call the police!	Chiamate la polizia!	kee-ah-**mah**-teh lah poh-lee-zee-ah
Call the emergency medical service!	Chiamate il pronto soccorso!	kee-ah-**mah**-teh eel pron-toh sohk-**kor**-soh
Call the fire department!	Chiamate i pompieri!	kee-ah-**mah**-teh ee pom-pee-**yeh**-ree
I lost my passport.	Ho perso il mio passaporto.	oh per-soh eel mee-oh pahs-sah-**por**-toh
My bag was stolen.	Mi hanno rubato la borsa.	mee ahn-noh roo-**bah**-toh lah bor-sah
Thief!	Ladro!	lah-droh
There's been an accident.	C'è stato un incidente.	chay stah-toh oon een-chee-**den**-teh
I've been mugged.	Sono stato assalito.	soh-noh stah-toh ahs-sah-**lee**-toh
Where is the embassy?	Dov'è l'ambasciata?	doh-vay lahm-bah-**shah**-tah

Verbs at a Glance

Effective use of verbs greatly enhances your communication skills. The following tables offer an overview of Italian verb conjugations, both regular and irregular, some of which have been presented throughout the book. If nothing else, verb tables can also serve as an effective sleeping aid during *le ore piccole* (the wee hours). *Sogni d'oro!*

Regular Verbs

After you have mastered the following regular verbs, you will be ready to use all of the tenses. Consult *501 Italian Verbs* (Barron's, 1992) or a similar text for a more comprehensive list.

Infinito (Infinitive)	Presente (Present)	Passato Prossimo (Present Perfect)	Imperativo (Imperative)	Imperfetto (Imperfect)	Futuro (Future)	Condizionale (Conditional)	Congiuntivo (Subjunctive)	Passato (Remoto)
parlare (to speak)	parlo	ho parlato	*	parlavo	parlerò	parlerei	parli	parlai
	parli	hai parlato	parla	parlavi	parlerai	parleresti	parli	parlasti
	parla	ha parlato	parli	parlava	parlerà	parlerebbe	parli	parlò
	parliamo	abbiamo parlato	parliamo	parlavamo	parleremo	parleremmo	parliamo	parlammo
	parlate	avete parlato	parlate	parlavate	parlerete	parlereste	parliate	parlaste
	parlano	hanno parlato	parlino	parlavano	parleranno	parlerebbero	parlino	parlarono
scrivere (to write)	scrivo	ho scritto	*	scrivevo	scriverò	scriverei	scriva	scrissi
	scrivi	hai scritto	scrivi	scrivevi	scriverai	scriveresti	scriva	scrivesti
	scrive	ha scritto	scriva	scriveva	scriverà	scriverebbe	scriva	scrisse
	scriviamo	abbiamo scritto	scriviamo	scrivevamo	scriveremo	scriveremmo	scriviamo	scrivemmo
	scrivete	avete scritto	scrivete	scrivevate	scriverete	scrivereste	scriviate	scriveste
	scrivono	hanno scritto	scrivano	scrivevano	scriveranno	scriverebbero	scrivano	scrissero

Infinito (Infinitive)	Presente (Present)	Passato Prossimo (Present Perfect)	Imperativo (Imperative)	Imperfetto (Imperfect)	Futuro (Future)	Condizionale (Conditional)	Congiuntivo (Subjunctive)	Passato (Remoto)
partire (to depart)	parto	sono partito/a	*	partivo	partirò	partirei	parta	partii
	parti	sei partito/a	parti	partivi	partirai	partiresti	parta	partisti
	parte	è partito/a	parta	partiva	partirà	partirebbe	parta	partì
	partiamo	siamo partiti/e	partiamo	partivamo	partiremo	partiremmo	partiamo	partimmo
	partite	siete partiti/e	partite	partivate	partirete	partireste	partiate	partiste
	partono	sono partiti/e	partano	partivano	partiranno	partirebbero	partano	partirono
capire (to understand)	capisco	ho capito	*	capivo	capirò	capirei	capisca	capii
	capisci	hai capito	capisci	capivi	capirai	capiresti	capisca	capisti
	capisce	ha capito	capisca	capiva	capirà	capirebbe	capisca	capì
	capiamo	abbiamo capito	capiamo	capivamo	capiremo	capiremmo	capiamo	capimmo
	capite	avete capito	capite	capivate	capirete	capireste	capiate	capiste
	capiscono	hanno capito	capiscano	capivano	capiranno	capirebbero	capiscano	capirono

*There is no imperative in the first person.

Essere (to be), Avere (to have)

The irregular verbs *essere* and *avere* are used on their own and additionally serve as auxiliary (helping) verbs in compound tenses such as the *passato prossimo* (present perfect) and others.

Infinito (Infinitive)	Presente (Present)	Passato Prossimo (Present Perfect)	Imperativo (Imperative)	Imperfetto (Imperfect)	Futuro (Future)	Condizionale (Conditional)	Congiuntivo (Subjunctive)	Passato (Remoto)
essere (to be)	sono	sono stato/a	*	ero	sarò	sarei	sia	fui
	sei	sei stato/a	sii	eri	sarai	saresti	sia	fosti
	è	è stato/a	sia	era	sarà	sarebbe	sia	fu
	siamo	siamo stati/e	siamo	eravamo	saremo	saremmo	siamo	fummo
	siete	siete stati/e	siate	eravate	sarete	sareste	siate	foste
	sono	sono stati/e	siano	erano	saranno	sarebbero	siano	furono
avere (to have)	ho	ho avuto	*	avevo	avrò	avrei	abbia	ebbi
	hai	hai avuto	abbi	avevi	avrai	avresti	abbia	avesti
	ha	ha avuto	abbia	aveva	avrà	avrebbe	abbia	ebbe
	abbiamo	abbiamo avuto	abbiamo	avevamo	avremo	avremmo	abbiamo	avemmo
	avete	avete avuto	abbiate	avevate	avrete	avreste	abbiate	aveste
	hanno	hanno avuto	abbiano	avevano	avranno	avrebbero	abbiano	ebbero

There is no imperative in the first person.

Irregular Verbs

Italian possesses many irregular verbs. An irregular verb is just a verb that deviates from established verb patterns.

Infinito (Infinitive)	Presente (Present)	Passato Prossimo (Present Perfect)	Imperativo (Imperative)	Imperfetto (Imperfect)	Futuro (Future)	Condizionale (Conditional)	Congiuntivo (Subjunctive)	Passato (Remoto)
andare (to go)	vado	sono andato/a	*	andavo	andrò	andrei	vada	andai
	vai	sei andato/a	va	andavi	andrai	andresti	vada	andasti
	va	è andato/a	vada	andava	andrà	andrebbe	vada	andò
	andiamo	siamo andati/e	andiamo	andavamo	andremo	andremmo	andiamo	andammo
andate	siete andati/e		andate	andavate	andrete	andreste	andiate	andaste
	vanno	sono andati/e	vadano	andavano	andranno	andrebbero	vadano	andarono
dire (to say)	dico	ho detto	*	dicevo	dirò	direi	dica	dissi
	dici	hai detto	di'	dicevi	dirai	diresti	dica	dicesti
	dice	ha detto	dica	diceva	dirà	direbbe	dica	disse
	diciamo	abbiamo detto	diciamo	dicevamo	diremo	diremmo	diciamo	dicemmo
	dite	avete detto	dite	dicevate	direte	direste	diciate	diceste
	dicono	hanno detto	dicano	dicevano	diranno	direbbero	dicano	dissero

Infinito (Infinitive)	Presente (Present)	Passato Prossimo (Present Perfect)	Imperativo (Imperative)	Imperfetto (Imperfect)	Futuro (Future)	Condizionale (Conditional)	Congiuntivo (Subjunctive)	Passato (Remoto)
dovere (to have to/must)	devo	ho dovuto	no imperative	dovevo	dovrò	dovrei	debba (deva)	dovei/dovetti
	devi	hai dovuto		dovevi	dovrai	dovresti	debba (deva)	dovesti
	deve	ha dovuto		doveva	dovrà	dovrebbe	debba (deva)	dovè/dovette
	dobbiamo	abbiamo dovuto		dovevamo	dovremo	dovremmo	dobbiamo	dovemmo
	dovete	avete dovuto		dovevate	dovrete	dovreste	dobbiate	doveste
	devono	hanno dovuto		dovevano	dovranno	dovrebbero	debbano (devano)	doverono/dovettero
fare (to do/make)	faccio	ho fatto	*	facevo	farò	farei	faccia	feci
	fai	hai fatto	fa'	facevi	farai	faresti	faccia	facesti
	fa	ha fatto	fai	faceva	farà	farebbe	faccia	fece
	facciamo	abbiamo fatto	faccia	facevamo	faremo	faremmo	facciamo	facemmo
	fate	avete fatto	facciamo	facevate	farete	fareste	facciate	faceste
	fanno	hanno fatto	fate	facevano	faranno	farebbero	facciano	fecero
			facciano					

Infinito (Infinitive)	Presente (Present)	Passato Prossimo (Present Perfect)	Imperativo (Imperative)	Imperfetto (Imperfect)	Futuro (Future)	Condizionale (Conditional)	Congiuntivo (Subjunctive)	Passato (Remoto)
morire (to die)	muoio	sono morto/a	*	morivo	morirò	morirei	muoia	morii
	muori	sei morto/a	muori	morivi	morirai	moriresti	muoia	moristi
	muore	è morto/a	muoia	moriva	morirà	morirebbe	muoia	morì
	moriamo	siamo morti/e	moriamo	morivamo	moriremo	moriremmo	moriamo	morimmo
	morite	siete morti/e	morite	morivate	morirete	morireste	moriate	moriste
	muoiono	sono morti/e	muoiano	morivano	moriranno	morirebbero	muoiano	morirono
nascere (to be born)	nasco	sono nato/a	*	nascevo	nascerò	nascerei	nasca	nacqui
	nasci	sei nato/a	nasci	nascevi	nascerai	nasceresti	nasca	nascesti
	nasce	è nato/a	nasca	nasceva	nascerà	nascerebbe	nasca	nacque
	nasciamo	siamo nati/e	nasciamo	nascevamo	nasceremo	nasceremmo	nasciamo	nascemmo
	nascete	siete nati/e	nascete	nascevate	nascerete	nascereste	nasciate	nasceste
	nascono	sono nati/e	nascano	nascevano	nasceranno	nascerebbero	nascano	nacquero
potere (to be able)	posso	ho potuto	no imperative	potevo	potrò	potrei	possa	potei
	puoi	hai potuto		potevi	potrai	potresti	possa	potesti
	può	ha potuto		poteva	potrà	potrebbe	possa	poté
	possiamo	abbiamo potuto		potevamo	potremo	potremmo	possiamo	potemmo
	potete	avete potuto		potevate	potrete	potreste	possiate	poteste
	possono	hanno potuto		potevano	potranno	potrebbero	possano	poterono

Infinito (Infinitive)	Presente (Present)	Passato Prossimo (Present Perfect)	Imperativo (Imperative)	Imperfetto (Imperfect)	Futuro (Future)	Condizionale (Conditional)	Congiuntivo (Subjunctive)	Passato (Remoto)
rimanere (to remain)	rimango	sono rimasto/a	*	rimanevo	rimarrò	rimarrei	rimanga	rimasi
	rimani	sei rimasto/a	rimani	rimanevi	rimarrai	rimarresti	rimanga	rimanesti
	rimane	è rimasto/a	rimanga	rimaneva	rimarrà	rimarrebbe	rimanga	rimase
	rimaniamo	siamo rimasti/e	rimaniamo	rimanevamo	rimarremo	rimarremmo	rimaniamo	rimanemmo
	rimanete	siete rimasti/e	rimanete	rimanevate	rimarrete	rimarreste	rimaniate	rimaneste
	rimangono	sono rimasti/e	rimangano	rimanevano	rimarranno	rimarrebbero	rimangano	rimasero
salire (to go up)	salgo	sono salito/a	*	salivo	salirò	salirei	salga	salii
	sali	sei salito/a	sali	salivi	salirai	saliresti	salga	salisti
	sale	è salito/a	salga	saliva	salirà	salirebbe	salga	salì
	saliamo	siamo saliti/e	saliamo	salivamo	saliremo	saliremmo	saliamo	salimmo
	salite	siete saliti/e	salite	salivate	salirete	salireste	saliate	saliste
	salgono	sono saliti/e	salgano	salivano	saliranno	salirebbero	salgano	salirono
sapere (to know)	so	ho saputo	*	sapevo	saprò	saprei	sappia	seppi
	sai	hai saputo	sappi	sapevi	saprai	sapresti	sappia	sapesti
	sa	ha saputo	sappia	sapeva	saprà	saprebbe	sappia	seppe
	sappiamo	abbiamo saputo	sappiamo	sapevamo	sapremo	sapremmo	sappiamo	sapemmo
	sapete	avete saputo	sappiate	sapevate	saprete	sapreste	sappiate	sapeste
	sanno	hanno saputo	sappiano	sapevano	sapranno	saprebbero	sappiano	seppero

Infinito (Infinitive)	Presente (Present)	Passato Prossimo (Present Perfect)	Imperativo (Imperative)	Imperfetto (Imperfect)	Futuro (Future)	Condizionale (Conditional)	Congiuntivo (Subjunctive)	Passato (Remoto)
venire (to come)	vengo	sono venuto/a	*	venivo	verrò	verrei	venga	venni
	vieni	sei venuto/a	vieni	venivi	verrai	verresti	venga	venisti
	viene	è venuto/a	venga	veniva	verrà	verrebbe	venga	venne
	veniamo	siamo venuti/e	veniamo	venivamo	verremo	verremmo	veniamo	venimmo
	venite	siete venuti/e	venite	venivate	verrete	verreste	veniate	veniste
	vengono	sono venuti/e	vengano	venivano	verranno	verrebbero	vengano	vennero
volere (to want)	voglio	ho voluto	*	volevo	vorrò	vorrei	voglia	volli
	vuoi	hai voluto	vuoi	volevi	vorrai	vorresti	voglia	volesti
	vuole	ha voluto	voglia	voleva	vorrà	vorrebbe	voglia	volle
	vogliamo	abbiamo voluto	vogliamo	volevamo	vorremo	vorremmo	vogliamo	volemmo
	volete	avete voluto	vogliate	volevate	vorrete	vorreste	vogliate	voleste
	vogliono	hanno voluto	vogliano	volevano	vorranno	vorrebbero	vogliano	vollero

*There is no imperative in the first person.

Reflexive Verbs *(Verbi Reflessivi)*

All reflexive verbs use *essere* in compound tenses such as the *passato prossimo* (present perfect) and can be recognized by the *si* at the end. Reflexive verbs are conjugated according to regular rules and must include the following reflexive pronouns:

mi	myself	*ci*	ourselves
ti	yourself	*vi*	yourselves
si	himself, herself, yourself	*si*	themselves

Ex.: (Chiamarsi) Come si chiama? (How do you call yourself?)

Commonly used reflexive verbs include the following:

alzarsi	to get up	*laurearsi*	to graduate
annoiarsi	to become bored	*lavarsi*	to wash oneself
arrabbiarsi	to become angry	*mettersi*	to put on
chiamarsi	to call oneself	*radersi*	to shave
conoscersi	to know each other	*sentirsi*	to feel
divertirsi	to enjoy	*sposarsi*	to get married
fermarsi	to stop	*svegliarsi*	to wake up

Irregular Past Participles

This chart includes a quick review of the irregular past participles used in compound tenses such as the *passato prossimo*. Unless otherwise indicated, past participles are used in conjunction with the helping verb *avere*. Verbs with an asterisk (*) require *essere* as their helping verb.

Infinitive	Past Participle	Infinitive	Past Participle
aprire (to open)	*aperto*	*nascere* (to be born)	*nato* *
assumere (to hire)	*assunto*	*offendere* (to offend)	*offeso*
chiedere (to ask)	*chiesto*	*offrire* (to offer)	*offerto*
chiudere (to close)	*chiuso*	*piacere* (to please)	*piaciuto* *
correre (to run)	*corso*	*prendere* (to take)	*preso*
cuocere (to cook)	*cotto*	*rimanere* (to remain)	*rimasto* *
decidere (to decide)	*deciso*	*rispondere* (to respond)	*risposto*
dipingere (to paint)	*dipinto*	*rompere* (to break)	*rotto*
dire (to say)	*detto*	*scegliere* (to choose)	*scelto*
dividere (to divide)	*diviso*	*scendere* (to descend)	*sceso*
esprimere (to express)	*espresso*	*stare* (to be; stay)	*stato* *
essere (to be)	*stato*	*succedere* (to happen)	*successo*
fare (to do/make)	*fatto*	*vedere* (to see)	*visto/veduto*
leggere (to read)	*letto*	*venire* (to come)	*venuto* *
mettere (to put)	*messo*	*vincere* (to win)	*vinto*
morire (to die)	*morto* *	*vivere* (to live)	*vissuto*
muovere (to move)	*mosso*		

Idiomatic Expressions

Italian has many more idiomatic expressions than what I've included here. Think of this list as an *antipasto* to get you started.

Italian	English
Come va?	How is it going?
Va bene/male.	It's going well/badly.
Ma va!	Come on!
Dai!	Come on! You're kidding.
Basta!	Enough!
Che roba!	What stuff! (I don't believe it!)
Che schifo!	How disgusting! (slang)
Davvero?	Really?
D'accordo.	Agreed.
fare alla Romana	to go Roman (to go Dutch)
fare la doccia	to "do" (take) a shower
fare una foto	to "do" (take) a picture
fare le ore piccole	to do the wee hours (to burn the midnight oil)
fare lo spiritoso	to be spirited (a wise-guy)

Italian	English
fare un freddo cane	to be dog cold (really cold)
Lascia perdere/stare.	Forget it.
Magari!	Wouldn't that be nice!
Meno male!	Luckily!
Penso di sì/no.	I think so/not.
Per dire la verità	To tell the truth
Santo cielo!	Holy heaven! My goodness!
Senza dubbio.	Without a doubt.
Sul serio?	Really?
Vale la pena.	It's worth it.
Di mamma cè n'è una sola.	Of mothers, there is only one.
Manco per sogno!	In your dreams!
Non c'è altro.	That's all. Don't think about it.

Glossary

KEY All feminine nouns (f.), irregular masculine nouns (m.), and plural (pl.) nouns are indicated. Irregular past participles are given in parentheses.

English to Italian

A

able, to be (can) potere
about (approximately) circa
about (consists of) di
above, on sopra
accent l'accento
accident l'incidente (m.)
across attraverso
activity l'attività (f.)
address l'indirizzo
admission charge il prezzo d'entrata
adult l'adulto
advance, in in anticipo
adventure l'avventura (f.)
after dopo
afternoon il pomeriggio
again ancora, di nuovo
against contro
age l'età (f.)
agency l'agenzia (f.)
agreement l'accordo
air l'aria (f.)

air conditioning l'aria condizionata (f.)
airplane l'aereo
airport l'aeroporto
alarm clock la sveglia (f.)
alcoholic alcolico
alive vivo
allergic allergico
allergy l'allergia (f.)
alley il vicolo
alone solo
although benché, sebbene
always sempre
ambulance l'ambulanza (f.)
and e, ed (before vowels)
angry arrabbiato
animal l'animale (m.)
answer la risposta (f.)
antiques l'antiquariato
apartment l'appartamento
aperitif l'aperitivo
apologize, to scusarsi
appetizer l'antipasto
aquarium l'acquario

area l'area (f.)
area code il prefisso
arm il braccio (pl. le braccia)
around intorno a
arrival l'arrivo
art l'arte (f.)
artist l'artista (m./f.)
ashtray il portacenere (m.)
ask, to chiedere (chiesto)
aspirin l'aspirina (f.)
assistance l'assistenza (f.)
ATM il Bancomat
attention!/warning! attenzione!
aunt la zia (f.)
automobile la macchina (f.), l'automobile (f.), l'auto (f.)
autumn l'autunno (m.)
available disponibile
avalanche la valanga (f.)
avoid, to evitare
awaken, to svegliarsi
away via

B

baby il bambino
baby bottle il biberon (m.)
bachelor lo scapolo
back, behind indietro
backpack lo zaino
bad male
bag (purse) la borsa (f.)
baker il fornaio
balcony il balcone (m.)
bank la banca (f.)
bar il bar (m.)
barber il barbiere (m.)
bartender il/la barista (m./f.)
basement la cantina (f.)
basketball la pallacanestro, il basket
bathroom il bagno

battery la batteria (f.), la pila (f.)
bay la baia (f.)
be, to essere (stato), stare (stato)
beach la spiaggia (f.)
beard la barba (f.)
beauty la bellezza (f.)
because perché
bed il letto
beef il manzo
beer la birra (f.)
before prima
begin, to iniziare, cominciare
behind dietro
bell la campana (f.)
beneath sotto
berth la cuccetta (f.)
beside, next to accanto a
best wishes! auguri!
better meglio
between tra
beverage la bibita (f.)
big, large grande
bill il conto
bird l'uccello
birth la nascita (f.)
birthday il compleanno
bishop il vescovo
bitter amaro
blanket la coperta (f.)
blood il sangue (m.)
blouse la camicetta (f.)
boarding l'imbarco
boat la barca (f.)
body il corpo
book il libro
bookstore la libreria (f.)
boot lo stivale (m.)
border la frontiera (f.)
boring noioso
boss il padrone/la padrona (f.)
both entrambi, tutt'e due

bottle   la bottiglia (f.)
bottom   il fondo
boulevard   il viale (m.)
bowl   la ciotola (f.);
la scodella (f.)
box   la scatola (f.)
boy   il ragazzo
brand   la marca (f.)
bread   il pane (m.)
breakdown   il guasto
breakfast   la prima
colazione (f.)
bridge   il ponte (m.)
broken   rotto
brother   il fratello
brother-in-law   il cognato
brown   castano, marrone
bruise   la contusione (f.),
il livido
building   l'edificio, il palazzo
bus   l'autobus (m.), la corriera (f.), il pullman (m.)
busy   impegnato, occupato
butcher shop   la macelleria
(f.)
button   il bottone (m.)
buy, to   comprare
by   da, in

(

cabin   la cabina (f.)
cable   il cavo
cable car   la funivia (f.)
cafeteria   la mensa (f.)
call, to   chiamare
camera   la macchina
fotografica (f.)
can opener   l'apriscatole
candle   la candela (f.)
car   *See* automobile.
car rental   l'autonoleggio
carafe   la caraffa (f.)

card   la carta (f.)
careful   attento
cash   i contanti (m. pl.)
cash register   la cassa (f.)
castle   il castello
cat   il gatto
cathedral   la cattedrale (f.)
Catholic   cattolico
cave   la grotta (f.)
ceiling   il soffitto
center   il centro
central   centrale
century   il secolo
certain   certo
chair   la sedia (f.)
change, to   cambiare
channel   il canale (m.)
chapel   la cappella (f.)
check   l'assegno
check, to   controllare
cheese   il formaggio
choose, to   scegliere (scelto)
Christian   cristiano
Christmas, Merry   Natale,
Buon
church   la chiesa (f.)
circle   il circolo
citizen   il cittadino/
la cittadina (f.)
citizenship   la cittadinanza (f.)
city   la città
clean, to   pulire
clear   chiaro
clever   furbo (slang),
intelligente
clock   l'orologio
closed   chiuso
clothing   l'abbigliamento
coast   la costa (f.)
coat   il cappotto,
il giubbotto
coffee   il caffè (m.)
coin   la moneta (f.)

colander il colapasta (m.)
cold freddo (adj.), il raffreddore (m.)
color il colore (m.)
come, to venire
community la comunità (f.)
company l'azienda (f.), la ditta (f.), la società (f.)
concert il concerto
condom il profilattico, il preservativo
conference la conferenza (f.), il congresso
conflict il conflitto
connection la coincidenza (f.)
contact il contatto
contest il concorso, la gara (f.)
contraceptive il contraccettivo
convenient comodo, pratico
conversation la conversazione (f.)
cook, to cucinare, cuocere (cotto)
cooked cotto
copy la copia (f.)
cork il tappo
corkscrew il cavatappi (m.)
corn il mais (m.)
cornmeal la polenta (f.)
correct corretto, a posto
cosmetics shop la profumeria (f.)
cost il costo, il prezzo
cost, to costare
costly costoso
count il conte, il conto
count, to contare
counter il banco, lo sportello
country la campagna (f.), il paese (m.)

couple la coppia (f.)
course il corso
court la corte (f.)
cousin il cugino/la cugina (f.)
cover charge il coperto
cow la vacca (f.)
crazy matto, pazzo
cream la crema (f.), la panna (f.)
create, to creare
credit il credito
credit card la carta di credito (f.)
crib la culla (f.)
cross la croce (f.)
crowded affollato
cruise la crociera (f.)
culture la cultura (f.)
cup la coppa (f.), la tazza (f.)
currency la valuta (f.), la moneta (f.)
current event l'attualità (f.)
curtain la tenda (f.)
curve la curva (f.)
customs la dogana (f.)
cute, pretty carino
cutting board il tagliere (m.)
cycling il ciclismo

D

daddy papà, babbo
dairy store la latteria (f.)
dam la diga (f.)
damaged danneggiato
dance il ballo, la danza (f.)
danger il pericolo
dangerous pericoloso
dark il buio, scuro (adj.)
darn! accidenti!
date la data (f.)
daughter la figlia (f.)

daughter-in-law la nuora (f.)
day il giorno, la giornata
dead morto
dear caro
death la morte (f.)
decision la decisione (f.)
degree il grado (temp.), la laurea (f.) (diploma)
delicious delizioso
dentist il/la dentista (m./f.)
depart, to partire
department il dipartimento
department store il grande magazzino
departure la partenza (f.)
desk la scrivania (f.)
dessert il dolce
destination la destinazione (f.)
detergent il detersivo
detour la deviazione (f.)
diabetes il diabete (m.)
diaper il pannolino
dictionary il dizionario
diet la dieta (f.)
different differente, diverso
difficult difficile
dining room la sala da pranzo (f.)
dinner la cena (f.)
dinner plate il piatto
direct diretto
direction la direzione (f.), l'indicazione (f.)
director il direttore/la direttrice (f.), il/la regista (m./f.)
dirty sporco
discount lo sconto
distance la distanza (f.)
distracted distratto
divorced divorziato
do, to fare (fatto)

doctor il dottore/la dottoressa (f.), il medico
document il documento
dog il cane (m.)
dome la cupola (f.), il duomo
door la porta (f.)
doorbell il campanello
down giù
drawing il disegno
dress il vestito
drive, to guidare
driver's license la patente (f.)
drug la droga (f.)
drugstore la drogheria (f.)
dry asciutto, secco
dry cleaner la lavanderia a secco, la tintoria (f.)
during durante, mentre

E

each ciascuno, ogni, ognuno
earrings gli orecchini (m. pl.)
earth la terra (f.)
east est, Oriente
Easter Monday lunedì dell'Angelo, Pasquetta (f.)
Easter, Happy Pasqua, Buona
easy facile
eat, to mangiare
eat breakfast, to fare la prima colazione
eat dinner, to cenare
eat lunch, to pranzare
egg l'uovo (pl. le uova)
election l'elezione (f.)
electricity l'elettricità (f.)
elevator l'ascensore (m.)
embassy l'ambasciata (f.)
emergency l'emergenza (f.)
emigrate, to emigrare
empty vuoto
end la fine (f.)

enemy il nemico
English inglese
engraved inciso
enough abbastanza, basta!
enter, to entrare
entrance l'entrata (f.), l'ingresso
envelope la busta (f.)
Epiphany (Jan. 6) la Befana (f.), l'Epifania (f.)
error l'errore (m.)
escape, to scappare
essential essenziale
even persino
evening la sera (f.), la serata
event l'avvenimento, l'evento
every ogni
everybody ognuno
everyone tutti
everything, all tutto
everywhere dappertutto
exactly esattamente
excellent eccellente, ottimo
exchange il cambio, lo scambio
exchange, to scambiare
excursion l'escursione (f.), la gita (f.)
excuse me! permesso!
exercise la ginnastica (f.)
exit l'uscita (f.)
expense la spesa (f.)
expensive caro
experience l'esperienza (f.)
export, to esportare
express espresso
eyeglasses gli occhiali (m. pl.)

F

fabric la stoffa (f.), il tessuto
face la faccia (f.), il viso

factory la fabbrica (f.)
faith la fede (f.)
fall in love, to innamorarsi
fall, to cadere
family la famiglia (f.)
far lontano
fare la tariffa (f.)
farm la fattoria (f.)
farmer il contadino
fat grasso
father il padre (m.)
father-in-law il suocero
faucet il rubinetto
fear la paura (f.)
Feast of the Assumption l'Assunzione (f.)
feel, to sentirsi
feeling il sentimento, la sensazione (f.)
ferry il traghetto
fever la febbre (f.)
fiancé il fidanzato
fiancée la fidanzata (f.)
field il campo, il prato
fill up, to (a gas tank) fare il pieno
film il film (m.), la pellicola (f.), il rullino
finally finalmente
finance la finanza (f.)
find, to trovare
finger il dito (pl. le dita)
finish, to finire
fire il fuoco
firefighter il pompiere (m.), il vigile del fuoco
fireplace il caminetto
first primo
first aid pronto soccorso
fish il pesce (m.)
flight il volo
floor il pavimento, il piano

Florence Firenze
flour la farina (f.)
flower il fiore (m.)
flu l'influenza (f.)
fly la mosca (f.)
fog la nebbia (f.)
food il cibo
foot il piede (m.)
for per
foreigner lo straniero/la straniera (f.)
forest la foresta (f.)
fork la forchetta (f.)
forward avanti
fountain la fontana (f.)
fragile fragile
free libero
free of charge gratis
fresh fresco
fried fritto
friend l'amico/l'amica (f.)
friendship l'amicizia (f.)
from di, da
fruit la frutta (f.)
full pieno
funny buffo
fur la pelliccia (f.)
furnishings l'arredamento
future il futuro

G

game il gioco, la partita (f.)
game room la sala giochi (f.)
garage il garage (m.)
garden il giardino, l'orto
garlic l'aglio
gas pump il distributore di benzina
gas tank il serbatoio
gasoline la benzina (f.)
gate il cancello

gift il regalo, il dono
girl la ragazza (f.)
give, to dare
glad contento
gladly! volentieri!
glass (drinking) il bicchiere (m.)
glass (material) il vetro
gloves i guanti (m. pl.)
go, to andare
god il dio
goddess la dea (f.)
gold l'oro
good buono
government il governo
gram il grammo
granddaughter la nipote (f.)
grandfather il nonno
grandmother la nonna (f.)
grandson il nipote (m.)
grapes l'uva (f.)
greengrocer's il fruttivendolo
greet, to salutare
grilled alla griglia
groceries gli alimentari (m. pl.)
ground la terra
ground floor il pianterreno
group il gruppo
guest l'ospite (m./f.)
guide la guida (f.)
gym la palestra (f.)

H

hair il pelo
hair (on head) i capelli (m. pl.)
hair dryer il fon (m.)
half la metà, mezzo (adj.)
hall la sala (f.)
hand la mano (f.) (pl. le mani)
handle la maniglia (f.)

hanger la gruccia (f.), la stampella (f.)

happen, to capitare, succedere (successo)

happy allegro, felice

Happy Birthday! Buon Compleanno!

Happy Easter! Buona Pasqua!

Happy Holidays! Buone Feste!

Happy New Year! Buon Anno!

harbor il porto

hard duro

hat il cappello

have to, to (must) dovere

have, to avere

hazel nut la nocciola (f.)

he lui, egli

head la testa (f.)

health la salute (f.)

healthy sano

hear, to sentire, udire

heart attack l'infarto

heat il riscaldamento

heavy pesante

hectogram l'ettogrammo (abbr. l'etto)

height l'altezza (f.)

hello ciao, buon giorno; pronto! (telephone)

helmet il casco, l'elmetto

help! aiuto!

here ecco, qua, qui

highway l'autostrada (f.)

hill la collina (f.)

history la storia (f.)

holiday la festa (f.)

homemade della casa, fatto in casa

honest onesto

honey il miele (m.)

honeymoon la luna di miele (f.)

hope la speranza (f.)

hospital l'ospedale

hostel l'ostello

hot caldo

hotel l'albergo, l'hotel (m.)

hour l'ora (f.)

house la casa (f.)

housewife la casalinga (f.)

how come

how much? quanto?

human l'umano

humble umile

humidity l'umidità (f.)

humor l'umore

hunger la fame (f.)

husband il marito

I

I io

ice il ghiaccio

ice-cream il gelato

ice-cream parlor la gelateria (f.)

identification card la carta d'identità (f.)

if se

ignorant ignorante

illness la malattia (f.)

image l'immagine (f.)

imagination l'immaginazione (f.)

imitation l'imitazione

immediately subito

immigration l'immigrazione (f.)

imperfect l'imperfetto

import, to importare

important importante

impossible impossibile

in   a, in
in a hurry   in fretta
in care of (c/o)   presso
in front of   davanti a
in season   della stagione
incredible   incredibile
indirect   indiretto
indoor   dentro, al coperto
industry   l'industria (f.)
inexpensive   economico
infection   l'infezione (f.)
inferior   inferiore
inform, to   informare
information   l'informazione (f.)
information office   l'ufficio informazioni
ingredient   l'ingrediente (m.)
inhabitant   l'abitante (m./f.)
injury   la ferita (f.)
inn   la pensione (f.), la locanda (f.)
insect   l'insetto
insect bite   la puntura (f.)
inside   dentro
instead   invece
insulin   l'insulina (f.)
insurance   l'assicurazione (f.)
intelligent   intelligente
interesting   interessante
intermission   l'intermezzo, l'intervallo
interpreter   l'interprete
introduce, to   introdurre (introdotto)
invitation   l'invito
invite, to   invitare
is   è
island   l'isola (f.)
Italian   italiano
Italy   l'Italia (f.)
itinerary   l'itinerario

J

jack (car)   il cric (m.)
jacket   la giacca (f.)
jail   il carcere (m.)
jeans   i jeans (m. pl.)
Jesus   Gesù
jeweler's   l'oreficeria (f.)
jewelry store   la gioielleria (f.)
Jewish   ebreo
journalist   il/la giornalista (m./f.)
juice   il succo
just   giusto, proprio

K

key   la chiave (f.)
kilogram   il chilogrammo (abbr. il chilo)
kilometer   il chilometro
kind   gentile
kindness   la gentilezza (f.)
king   il rè
kiss   il bacio
knife   il coltello
know, to (someone)   conoscere (conosciuto)
know, to (something)   sapere
kosher   kasher

L

lace   il merletto
lake   il lago
lamb   l'agnello
lamp   la lampada (f.)
landlord   il padrone di casa
lane   la corsia (f.)
language   la lingua (f.)
large   grande, grosso
last   scorso, ultimo
late   tardi

laundry il bucato
laundry service la lavanderia (f.)
law il Diritto, la giurisprudenza (f.), la legge (f.)
lawyer l'avvocato
lazy pigro
leaf la foglia (f.)
learn, to imparare
leather il cuoio, la pelle (f.)
leave, to (depart) partire
leave, to (behind) lasciare
left sinistro
leg la gamba (f.)
length la lunghezza (f.)
less meno
lesson la lezione (f.)
letter la lettera (f.)
license la patente (f.)
license plate la targa (f.)
life la vita (f.)
light la luce (f.)
lightning flash il lampo
line la linea (f.)
lip il labbro
list l'elenco
liter il litro
literature la letteratura (f.)
little piccolo, (a little) un po'
live, to abitare, vivere (vissuto)
living room il salotto, il soggiorno
local locale
lodge, to alloggiare
long lungo
look, to guardare
lose, to perdere (perso)
lost and found l'ufficio oggetti smarriti
lotion la lozione (f.)
love l'amore (m.)

lunch il pranzo
luxury lusso

M

magazine la rivista (f.)
magic la magia (f.)
magnificent magnifico
maid la domestica (f.)
mail la posta (f.)
mail, to inviare, spedire
mailbox la cassetta postale (f.)
man l'uomo
management l'amministrazione (f.)
manager il/la dirigente (m./f.)
manufacture, to fabbricare
map la carta (f.), la mappa (f.)
marble il marmo
marina la marina (f.), il lido
market il mercato
married sposato
masculine maschile
mass la messa (f.)
matches i fiammiferi (m. pl.)
maybe forse
mayor il sindaco
me mi, a me
meal il pasto
meaning il significato, il senso
measure la misura (f.)
meat la carne (f.)
mechanic il meccanico
medicine la medicina (f.)
meet, to incontrare
meeting il congresso, la riunione (f.)
menu la lista (f.), il menù
merchandise la merce (f.)
merchant il/la mercante (m./f.)

message   il messaggio
messenger   il corriere
metal   il metallo
midnight   la mezzanotte (f.)
mile   il miglio (pl. le miglia)
milk   il latte (m.)
mind   la mente (f.)
minister   il ministro
minority   la minoranza (f.)
minute   il minuto
mirror   lo specchio
Miss, young lady   la signorina (f.)
model   il modello
modern   moderno
modest   modesto
moment   l'attimo, il momento
monastery   il monastero
money   il denaro, i soldi (m. pl.)
money exchange office   l'ufficio cambio
money order   il vaglia postale (m.)
month   il mese (m.)
monument   il monumento
moon   la luna (f.)
more   più
more than, in addition to   oltre
morning   la mattina (f.)
morsel, nibble   il bocconcino
mosaic   il mosaico
mosquito   la zanzara (f.)
mother   la madre (f.)
mother-in-law   la suocera (f.)
motor   il motore (m.)
motorcycle   la motocicletta (f.)
mountain   la montagna (f.)
mouth   la bocca (f.)

movie   il film
Mr.   il signore (m.)
Mrs.   la signora (f.)
museum   il museo
music   la musica (f.)
musician   il/la musicista (m./f.)
Muslim   mussulmano
mustard   la senape (f.)
myth   il mito

N

name   il nome (m.)
name of spouse   il nome del coniuge
napkin   la salvietta (f.), il tovagliolo
nationality   la nazionalità (f.)
native language   la madrelingua (f.)
natural   naturale
nausea   la nausea (f.)
near   vicino
necessary   necessario
necessity   la necessità (f.)
necklace   la collana (f.)
need, I   ho bisogno
neighbor   il vicino/la vicina (f.)
neighborhood   il quartiere (m.)
neither   neppure
neither ... nor   né ... né
nephew   il nipote
nervous   nervoso
never   mai
new   nuovo
news   la notizia (f.)
newspaper   il giornale (m.), il quotidiano
newspaper vendor   il giornalaio
newsstand   l'edicola (f.)

next prossimo

nice simpatico

niece la nipote (f.)

night la notte (f.)

no entrance vietato l'ingresso

no one nessuno

no parking divieto di sosta

noisy rumoroso

noon mezzogiorno

normal normale

north nord

not non

notebook il quaderno

nothing niente, nulla

noun il nome (m.)

novel il romanzo

now adesso, ora

number il numero

nurse l'infermiera (f.)

O

occupied occupato

ocean l'oceano

of di

offer l'offerta (f.)

office l'ufficio

often spesso

oil l'olio

old vecchio

olive l'oliva (f.)

on su

on board a bordo

one-way street senso unico

only solamente

open aperto

opinion l'opinione (f.)

opposite il contrario; opposto

optician l'ottico

or o, oppure

original originale

outdoor all'aperto

outfit l'abito

outside fuori

oven il forno

overcoat il cappotto, il soprabito

overdone scotto, troppo cotto

owner il proprietario

P

package il pacco

pain il dolore (m.)

paint la vernice (f.)

painter il pittore/la pittrice (f.)

painting la pittura (f.), il quadro

pair il paio (pl. le paia)

pan la padella (f.)

pants i pantaloni (m. pl.)

paper la carta (f.)

paradise il paradiso

parents i genitori (m. pl.)

park il parco

parking lot il parcheggio

passport il passaporto

pastry shop la pasticceria (f.)

path il sentiero, la via (f.)

payment il pagamento

peace la pace (f.)

peanut la nocciolina (f.)

pen la penna (f.)

penalty la multa (f.), la pena (f.)

pencil la matita (f.)

people la gente (f.)

pepper il pepe (m.)

percentage il percento, la percentuale (f.)

perfume il profumo

person la persona (f.)
pharmacy la farmacia (f.)
photocopy la fotocopia (f.)
photograph la fotografia (f.)
phrase la frase (f.)
piece il pezzo
pill la pillola (f.)
pillow il cuscino
pink rosa
place il locale (m.), il luogo, il posto
plain la pianura (f.)
plan il programma (m.)
plant la pianta (f.)
plate il piatto
please per favore, per piacere
pleasing piacevole
pocket la tasca (f.)
poem, poetry la poesia (f.)
poet il poeta (m.), la poetessa (f.)
poison il veleno
police la polizia (f.)
police headquarters la questura (f.)
police officer il carabiniere (m.), il poliziotto, il vigile
political party il partito
politics la politica (f.)
pollution l'inquinamento
pond lo stagno
poor povero
Pope il Papa (m.)
population la popolazione (f.)
pork il maiale (m.), il porco
portion la porzione (f.)
portrait il ritratto
post office l'ufficio postale
postage stamp il francobollo
postal carrier il postino
postcard la cartolina (f.)

pot la pentola (f.)
poultry il pollame (m.)
poverty la miseria (f.), la povertà (f.)
practice la pratica (f.)
prayer la preghiera (f.)
pregnant incinta
prescription la ricetta (f.)
present il presente
preservatives i conservanti (m. pl.)
price il prezzo
priest il prete (m.)
print la stampa (f.)
printing la tipografia (f.)
prison il carcere (m.), la prigione (f.)
private property la proprietà privata (f.)
problem il problema (m.)
product il prodotto
production la produzione (f.)
profession la professione (f.)
progress il progresso
prohibited vietato, proibito
project il progetto
pronunciation la pronuncia (f.)
Protestant protestante
proud orgoglioso
psychology la psicologia (f.)
public il pubblico
publicity la pubblicità (f.)
pupil l'allievo, lo scolaro
pure puro
purple viola
purse la borsa (f.)

Q

quality la qualità (f.)
quantity la quantità (f.)

queen la regina (f.)
question, to domandare
quickly, early presto
quit, to smettere (smesso)

R

rabbi il rabbino
race la corsa (f.)
radio la radio (f.)
rail car il vagone (m.)
railroad la ferrovia (f.)
rain la pioggia (f.)
raincoat l'impermeabile (m.)
rare raro, al sangue
raw crudo
razor il rasoio
ready pronto
receipt la ricevuta (f.), lo scontrino
recent recente
reception il ricevimento
recipe la ricetta (f.)
record il disco
red rosso
refreshment la bevanda (f.)
refrigerator il frigorifero
refund il rimborso
region la regione (f.)
relationship il rapporto
relative il/la parente (m./f.)
religion la religione (f.)
remainder il resto
Renaissance il Rinascimento
rent l'affitto
rent, to affittare, noleggiare
repair, to riparare
repeat, to ripetere
reservation la prenotazione (f.)
reserve, to prenotare
reserved riservato

reservoir la riserva d'acqua (f.)
residence il domicilio, la residenza (f.)
resident l'abitante (m./f.)
responsible responsabile
restaurant il ristorante (m.)
result il risultato
return, to ritornare, tornare
rice il riso
rich ricco
right (direction) destro
right (legal) il diritto
ring l'anello
ripe maturo
river il fiume (m.)
robbery la rapina (f.)
rock la pietra (f.), la roccia (f.)
roll of film il rullino
romantic romantico
roof il tetto
room la camera (f.), la stanza (f.)
root la radice (f.)
rope la corda (f.)
round-trip (ticket) il biglietto d'andata e ritorno
route il percorso, la via
row la fila (f.)
ruckus il baccano
ruins le rovine (f. pl.)
rush hour l'ora di punta (f.)

S

sad triste
safe sicuro
sailboat la barca a vela (f.)
saint il santo/la santa (f.)
salad l'insalata (f.)
sale i saldi (m. pl.), la svendita (f.)

sales clerk il commesso/la commessa (f.)

salt il sale (m.)

same stesso

sand la sabbia (f.)

sandwich il panino

sanitary napkin l'assorbente (m.)

sauce la salsa (f.)

say, to dire (detto)

scarf la sciarpa (f.)

schedule l'orario, la tabella (f.)

school la scuola (f.)

science la scienza (f.)

scissors le forbici (f. pl.)

scooter il motorino

screwdriver il cacciavite (m.)

sculpture la scultura (f.)

sea il mare (m.)

sea shell la conchiglia (f.)

season la stagione (f.)

seat il posto, il sedile

seat belt la cintura di sicurezza (f.)

second secondo

see you later! arrivederci! ci vediamo!

see, to vedere (visto)

send, to inviare, mandare, spedire

sentence la frase (f.)

separated separato

serious grave, serio

service il servizio

set fisso, fissato

sex il sesso

she lei, ella

sheet il lenzuolo

sheet of paper il foglio

ship la nave (f.)

shirt la camicia (f.)

shoe la scarpa (f.)

shoe store la calzoleria (f.)

shop la bottega (f.), il negozio

shop window la vetrina (f.)

short basso, corto

shorts i calzoncini (m. pl.)

show lo spettacolo, la mostra (f.) (art)

shower la doccia (f.)

shrimp il gambero

Sicily la Sicilia

sick ammalato

side dish il contorno

sidewalk il marciapiede (m.)

sign il cartello, il segno

signal il segnale (m.)

signature la firma (f.)

silence il silenzio

silk la seta (f.)

silver l'argento

singer il/la cantante (m./f.)

single singolo

single room il monolocale (m.)

sink il lavandino

sister la sorella (f.)

sister-in-law la cognata (f.)

size la misura (f.), la taglia (f.)

sketch lo schizzo

skiing lo sci (m.)

skirt la gonna (f.)

sky il cielo

sleep il sonno

sleep, to dormire

sleeping pill il sonnifero

slide la diapositiva (f.)

slow down rallentare

small piccolo

smoke, to fumare

snack lo spuntino

snow la neve (f.)

so-so così così

soap il sapone (m.)

soccer il calcio, il football

soccer player il calciatore (m.)

socks le calze (f. pl.), i calzini (m. pl.)

sofa il divano

soft soffice

sold out esaurito

soldier il soldato

some alcuni/alcune, qualche

someone qualcuno

something qualcosa

sometimes qualche volta, talvolta

son il figlio

son-in-law il genero

soon subito, presto

soul l'anima (f.)

soup la minestra (f.), la zuppa (f.)

south sud

space lo spazio

sparkling wine lo spumante (m.)

special speciale

spicy piccante

spiritual spirituale

splendid splendido

spoiled guasto, rovinato

sponge la spugna (f.)

spoon il cucchiaio

sport lo sport (m.)

sports ground il campo sportivo

spouse lo sposo/la sposa (f.)

spring la sorgente (f.), la primavera (f.) (season)

squid i calamari (m. pl.)

stadium lo stadio

stage il palcoscenico

stain la macchia (f.)

stairs la scala (f.), le scale (f. pl.)

star la stella (f.)

station la stazione (f.)

stationery store la cartoleria (f.)

statue la statua (f.)

steak la bistecca (f.)

stepfather il patrigno

stepsister la sorellastra (f.)

stewardess la hostess (f.)

still (again) ancora

stockings le calze (f. pl.), i collant

stomach lo stomaco, la pancia

stop la fermata (f.)

stop, to fermare

storm la tempesta (f.)

story la storia (f.)

stove burner il fornello

straight diritto

strange strano

straw (drinking) la cannuccia (f.)

stream (brook) il ruscello, il corso d'acqua

street la strada (f.), la via (f.)

stress lo stress

strong forte

student lo studente/la studentessa (f.)

stuff la roba (f.)

stuffed ripieno

stupid stupido

suburbs la periferia (f.)

subway la metropolitana (f.)

sugar lo zucchero

suit l'abito, il vestito

summer l'estate (f.)

sun il sole (m.)

sunrise l'alba (f.)

sunset   il tramonto
supermarket   il supermercato
swamp   la palude (f.)
sweater   la maglia (f.)
sweet   dolce
swimming pool   la piscina (f.)
symphony   la sinfonia (f.)
synagogue   la sinagoga (f.)
synthetic   sintetica

T

table   il tavolo (restaurant),
la tavola
tablecloth   la tovaglia (f.)
tablet   la compressa (f.)
tailor   il sarto
tall   alto
tape   l'adesivo, il nastro
taste   il gusto, il sapore (m.)
taste, a   un assaggio
tax   la tassa (f.)
taxi   il tassì
taxi meter   il tassametro
tea   il tè (m.)
teacher   l'insegnante (m./f.)
teaspoon   il cucchiaino
telephone   il telefono
telephone call   la telefonata
(f.)
telephone card   la carta
telefonica (f.)
telephone, to   telefonare
tell, to   dire (detto), raccon-
tare
terrace   il terrazzo
thank you!   grazie!
that   quello/quella
theater   il teatro
then   allora, poi
there   ci, lià / là
there is   c'è

thermometer   il termometro
they   loro
thief   il ladro
thin   magro
thing   la cosa (f.)
thirst   la sete (f.)
this   questo
this evening   stasera
this morning   stamattina
thunder   il tuono
ticket   il biglietto
ticket counter   la biglietteria (f.)
tide   la marea (f.)
tie   la cravatta (f.)
tight   stretto
tile   la piastrella (f.)
time   l'ora (f.), il tempo
tip   la mancia (f.)
tire   il pneumatico
tired   stanco
tissue   il fazzoletto
to   a, in
tobacco shop   la tabaccheria
(f.)
today   oggi
together   insieme
toilet   il gabinetto, la toilette
(f.)
toilet paper   la carta igienica
(f.)
toll   il pedaggio
toll-free number   il numero
verde
tomato   il pomodoro
tomorrow   domani
tonight   stanotte
too   troppo
tooth   il dente (m.)
toothbrush   lo spazzolino da
denti
toothpaste   il dentifricio

total totale
tour il giro
tourism il turismo
tourist il/la turista (m./f.)
toward verso
town square la piazza (f.)
toy il giocattolo
track il binario
traffic il traffico
traffic light il semaforo
train il treno
translation la traduzione (f.)
transport, to trasportare
trash i rifiuti (m. pl.)
trash can il bidone della spazzatura
travel, to viaggiare
tree l'albero
trip il viaggio
trouble il guaio
truck il camion (m.)
true vero
trust la fiducia (f.)
truth la verità (f.)
try, to provare
tub la vasca (f.)
tunnel la galleria (f.), il sotterraneo
turn il turno
turn off, to spegnere (spento)
type, kind la specie (f.), il tipo

U

ugly brutto
umbrella l'ombrello
uncle lo zio
uncomfortable scomodo
understood! capito!
underwear la biancheria intima (f.)

unemployed disoccupato
United States gli Stati Uniti (m. pl.)
unmarried celibe (m.), nubile (f.)
until fino a
urgent urgente
use, to usare

V

vacation la vacanza (f.)
vaccination la vaccinazione (f.)
validated convalidato
valise la valigia (f.)
variety la varietà (f.)
vase il vaso
VAT/sales tax I.V.A. (Imposta Valore Aggiunto)
vegetarian vegetariano
vehicle il veicolo
verb il verbo
very molto
victim la vittima (f.)
view la vista (f.)
villa la villa (f.)
village il villaggio
vinegar l'aceto
violence la violenza (f.)
visible visibile
visit la visita (f.)
visit, to visitare
vitamin la vitamina (f.)
vocabulary il vocabolario

W

wait, to aspettare
waiter il cameriere
waiting room la sala d'attesa (f.)
waitress la cameriera (f.)

walk, to camminare, passeggiare
wall il muro, la parete (f.)
wallet il portafoglio
want, to volere
war la guerra (f.)
warm caldo
warning l'avviso
wash, to lavare
watch l'orologio
water l'acqua (f.)
wave l'onda (f.)
weak debole
wear, to indossare, portare
weather il tempo
week la settimana (f.)
weekend il fine settimana
weigh, to pesare
weight il peso
welcome! greetings! benvenuto!
well (adv.) bene
well il pozzo
west ovest, l'Occidente
wet bagnato
what che, che cosa
wheel la ruota (f.)
when quando
where dove
wherever ovunque
which quale
while mentre
who chi
wholesale all'ingrosso
why perché
wife la moglie (f.)
wind il vento
window la finestra (f.), il finestrino
windshield il parabrezza (m.)
wine il vino

wine bar l'enoteca (f.)
winery l'azienda vinicola (f.)
winter l'inverno
wish il desiderio, la voglia (f.)
with con
within fra
without senza
woman la donna (f.), la femmina (f.), la signora (f.)
wood il legno
woods il bosco, la selva (f.)
wool la lana (f.)
work il lavoro
worker l'impiegato, l'operaio
world il mondo
worried preoccupato
worse peggio
write, to scrivere (scritto)
writer lo scrittore/la scrittrice (f.)
wrong, to be sbagliare

X-Y

year l'anno
yes sì
yesterday ieri
you Lei (polite), tu (familiar), voi (plural)
you are welcome! prego!
young giovane

Z

zero zero
zipper la cerniera (f.)
zoo lo zoo

Italian to English

A

a, ad (before vowels) at, in, to, by

a bordo on board

abbastanza enough

l'abbazia (f.) abbey

l'abbigliamento clothing

abbronzarsi to get tanned

l'abitante (m./f.) resident, inhabitant

abitare to live

l'abito outfit, suit

accanto a beside, next to

accendere (acceso) to light, to turn on

l'accento accent

l'accesso access

accidenti! darn!

accompagnare to accompany

accordo agreement

l'aceto vinegar

l'acqua (f.) water

acqua non potabile do not drink water

l'acquario aquarium

adesso now

l'adulto adult

l'aereo airplane

l'aeroporto airport

l'affare (m.) business, deal

affittare to rent

affittasi for rent

l'affitto rent

l'agenzia (f.) agency

aiuto! help!

al coperto indoor

al forno grilled

al sangue rare

l'alba (f.) sunrise

l'albergo hotel

l'albero tree

alcolico alcoholic

alcool alchohol (m.)

alcuni/alcune some

gli alimentari (m. pl.) groceries

all'aperto outdoor, open air

allegro happy

l'allergia (f.) allergy

allora then

almeno at least

altezza (f.) height

alto tall

altro other

alzare to raise, lift

alzarsi to get up

amare to love

amaro bitter

l'ambasciata (f.) embassy

l'ambulanza (f.) ambulance

l'amicizia (f.) friendship

l'amico/l'amica (f.) friend

ammalato sick, ill

l'amministrazione (f.) management, administration

l'amore (m.) love

anche also

ancora still, again, yet

andare to go

andata e ritorno round-trip (ticket)

l'anello ring

l'anima (f.) spirit

l'animale (m.) animal

l'anno year

l'annuncio announcement

antico ancient, antique

l'antipasto appetizer

antipatico unpleasant, disagreeable
anzi and even, but rather
anziano elderly
l'aperitivo aperitif
aperto open, (all'aperto) outside
aprire (aperto) to open
l'area (f.) area
l'aria (f.) aria, air, appearance
l'aria condizionata (f.) air conditioning
arrabbiato angry
l'arredamento furnishings
arrivare to arrive
arrivederci! see you later!
l'arrivo arrival
arrosto roasted
l'arte (f.) art
l'artista (m./f.) artist
l'ascensore (m.) elevator
asciutto dry
ascoltare to listen to
l'asilo kindergarten, day-care center
aspettare to wait for
assaggiare to taste
l'assegno check
l'assicurazione (f.) insurance
l'assistenza (medica) (f.) assistance, insurance (health)
l'Assunzione (f.) Feast of the Assumption
l'atleta (m./f.) athlete
attendere prego! please hold!
attenzione! attention! warning!
l'attimo moment
l'attività (f.) activity
attivo active
l'atto document, record
l'attore actor

attraverso across
l'attrice (f.) actress
auguri! best wishes!
l'autobus (m.) bus
l'automobile (f.) (abbr. auto) car
l'autonoleggio car rental
l'autostop (m.) hitchhiking
l'autostrada (f.) highway
l'autunno (m.) autumn
avanti forward
avere to have
avvenire to happen
l'avventura (f.) adventure
avvertire to warn
avvicinarsi to approach, to get near
l'avvocato lawyer
l'azienda (f.) firm, company
azzurro light blue

B

il babbo dad
baciare to kiss
il bacio kiss
bagnato wet
il bagno bath
la baia (f.) bay
il balcone (m.) balcony
il ballo dance
il bambino baby, child
la banca (f.) bank
la bancarella (f.) stall, booth
il banco counter
il Bancomat ATM
il bar (m.) bar, café
la barba (f.) beard
il barbiere (m.) barber
la barca (f.) boat
il/la barista (m./f.) bartender
la barzelletta (f.) joke

basso short, low
basta! enough!
la Befana (f.) Epiphany
(January 6)
la bellezza (f.) beauty
benché although
bene well
benvenuto! welcome!
la benzina (f.) gasoline
bere (bevuto) to drink
la bestia (f.) beast
la bevanda (f.) refreshment
la biancheria intima (f.)
underwear
la Bibbia (f.) Bible
il biberon (m.) baby bottle
la bibita (f.) refreshment,
beverage
il bicchiere (m.) glass
la biglietteria (f.) ticket
counter
il biglietto ticket
il binario track, platform
il bocconcino morsel, nibble
bordo, a aboard
la borsa (f.) bag, purse
il bosco woods
la bottega (f.) shop
il braccio arm
bravo good, able
breve brief, short
la brioche (f.) brioche,
croissant
il brodo broth
bruciato burnt
brutto ugly
il bucato laundry
buffo funny
il buio dark
Buon Anno! Happy New
Year!

Buon Compleanno! Happy
Birthday!
Buon giorno! Good day,
hello!
Buon Natale! Merry
Christmas!
Buona Feste! Happy
Holidays!
Buona Pasqua! Happy
Easter!
buono good
la bustina (f.) bag

C

c'è there is
il caffè (m.) coffee, café
i calamari (m. pl.) squid
il calcio soccer, kick
caldo heat, hot (adj.)
le calze (f. pl.) stockings
i calzini (m. pl.) socks
il calzolaio shoe repair
la calzoleria (f.) shoe store
i calzoncini (m. pl.) shorts
il cambio exchange
la camera (f.) room
la cameriera (f.) waitress,
maid
il cameriere waiter
la camicetta (f.) blouse
la camicia (f.) shirt
il caminetto fireplace
il camino chimney
il camion (m.) truck
camminare to walk
la campagna (f.) country,
countryside
il campanello doorbell
il campeggio camping
il campionato match,
championship

il **campo sportivo**   sports
ground
il **cancello**   gate
la **candela** (f.)   candle
il **candidato**   candidate
il **cane** (m.)   dog
il/la **cantante** (m./f.)   singer
i **capelli** (m. pl.)   hair (on
head)
capito!   understood!
la **cappella** (f.)   chapel
il **cappello**   hat
il **cappotto**   overcoat
il **carabiniere** (m.)   police
officer
la **caramella** (f.)   candy
il **carcere** (m.)   jail
carino   cute, pretty
la **carne** (f.)   meat
caro   dear, expensive
la **carta** (f.)   paper
la **carta di credito** (f.)
credit card
la **carta d'identità**   identification card
la **carta igienica** (f.)   toilet
paper
la **carta stradale** (f.)   map
la **carta telefonica** (f.)   telephone card
il **cartello**   sign
la **cartoleria** (f.)   stationery
store
la **cartolina** (f.)   postcard
la **casa** (f.)   house, home
il **casco**   helmet
la **cassa** (f.)   cash register
castano   brown
il **castello**   castle
la **cattedrale** (f.)   cathedral
cattivo   bad, evil, naughty
cattolico   Catholic

il **cavallo**   horse
il **cavatappi** (m.)   corkscrew
il **cavo**   cable
celibe   unmarried, single (m.)
la **cena** (f.)   dinner
cenare   to dine
il **centro**   center, downtown
cercare   to search, look for
il **certificato**   certificate
certo   certain, sure, of course!
che   what, who, which, that
che cosa   what
chi   who? whom? the one who
chiamare   to call
chiamarsi   to call oneself (to
be named)
chiaro   clear, light
la **chiave** (f.)   key
chiedere (chiesto)   to ask
la **chiesa** (f.)   church
il **chilogrammo**   kilogram
il **chilometro**   kilometer
chiudere (chiuso)   to close
chiuso   closed
la **chiusura festiva** (f.)
closed for the holidays
ci   there
ciascuno   each, each one
il **cibo**   food
il **cielo**   sky, heaven
la **ciliegia** (f.)   cherry
il **cinema** (m.)   cinema
la **cintura** (f.)   belt
la **cintura di sicurezza** (f.)
seat belt
ciò   that which
circa   about, approximately
la **città** (f.)   city
la **cittadinanza** (f.)   citizenship
il **cittadino/la cittadina** (f.)
citizen

classico classical

il/la cliente (m./f.) client, customer

la cognata (f.) sister-in-law

il cognato brother-in-law

il cognome (m.) surname

la coincidenza (f.) connection, coincidence

la colazione (f.) breakfast, lunch

la collana (f.) necklace

i collant (m. pl.) stockings

il/la collega (m./f.) colleague

la collina (f.) hill

il colore (m.) color

il coltello knife

il comandamento commandment

come how, like, as

cominciare to begin, to start

il commesso/la commessa (f.) sales clerk

comodo convenient, comfortable

il compleanno birthday

il complimento compliment

il comportamento behavior

comprare to buy

la comprensione (f.) understanding

la compressa (f.) tablet, pill

comunicare to communicate

la comunità (f.) community

comunque however, no matter how

con with

il concerto concert

la conchiglia (f.) sea shell

condividere (condiviso) to share

il conflitto conflict

il conforto comfort, convenience

congratulazioni! congratulations!

il congresso meeting, conference

conoscere (conosciuto) to know someone

consecutivo consecutive

la conseguenza (f.) consequence

i conservanti (m. pl.) preservatives

il contadino/la contadina (f.) farmer, peasant

i contanti (m. pl.) cash

il contatto contact

contento glad, satisfied

continuare to continue

il conto check, bill, account

il contorno side dish

il contraccettivo contraceptive

il contrario opposite

contro against

il controllo check, control

convalidare to validate

convalidato validated

il convento convent

la coperta (f.) blanket, cover

il coperto cover charge

la copia (f.) copy

la coppa (f.) cup

la coppia (f.) couple

il coro chorus, choir

il corpo body

corretto correct

il corriere messenger, courier

la corriera (f.) bus

la corsa (f.) race

la corsia (f.) lane

il corso course

cortese courteous
la cosa (f.) thing (Cosa c'è? What is it?)
così so, thus
così così so-so
la costa (f.) coast
il costo cost, price
costare to cost
costoso costly, expensive
cotto cooked
credere to believe
il credito credit
cristiano Christian
croccante crunchy
la croce (f.) cross
la crociera (f.) cruise
crudo raw, uncooked
la cuccetta (f.) berth
il cucchiaio spoon
cucinare to cook
il cugino/la cugina (f.) cousin
cui whom, that, which
la cultura (f.) culture
culturale cultural
cuocere (cotto) to cook
il cuoio leather
la cupola (f.) dome
curare to care for, to look after
la curva (f.) curve
il cuscino pillow

D

da from, by
danneggiato damaged
dappertutto everywhere
dare to give
la data (f.) date
davanti a in front of
davvero really
la dea (f.) goddess
decidere (deciso) to decide

definire to define
la definizione (f.) definition
il delfino dolphin
della casa homemade
della stagione in season
il denaro money
il dente (m.) tooth
il dentifricio toothpaste
il/la dentista (m./f.) dentist
dentro inside
il desiderio wish, desire
la destinazione (f.) destination
destro right
il detersivo detergent
la deviazione (f.) detour
di of, about, from
di solito usually
il dialogo dialogue
il diamante (m.) diamond
la diapositiva (f.) slide
dichiarare to declare
la didattica (f.) pedagogy, teaching
la dieta (f.) diet
dietro a behind
difendere (difeso) to defend
il difetto defect
la differenza (f.) difference
difficile difficult
la diga (f.) dam
la digestione (f.) digestion
diminuire to decrease
dinamico energetic
il dio god
dipendere (dipeso) to depend
dipingere (dipinto) to paint
dire (detto) to say, to tell
diretto direct
la direzione (f.) direction
dirigere (diretto) to manage, to direct
diritto straight (adv.)

il Diritto law
il discorso speech, discussion
la discussione (f.) discussion
disegnare to draw
il disegno drawing, design
la disgrazia (f.) misfortune
disoccupato unemployed
dispiacere (dispiaciuto) to be sorry
disponibile available
la distanza (f.) distance
il distributore di benzina gas pump
distruggere (distrutto) to destroy
la ditta (f.) firm, business
il divano sofa
diverso different
divertirsi to enjoy oneself
divieto di sosta no parking
divorziato divorced
il dizionario dictionary
la doccia (f.) shower
il documento document
la dogana (f.) customs
dolce sweet
il dolce dessert
il dollaro dollar
il dolore (m.) pain
domandare to question
domani tomorrow
la domestica (f.) maid
il domicilio residence
la donna (f.) woman
dopo after (prep.), afterward (adv.)
doppio double
dormire to sleep
dove where
dovere to have to, to must
la droga (f.) drug
il duomo cathedral, dome

dunque thus, then
durante during
duro hard, tough

E

e, ed (before vowels) and
è is
ebbene well then, so
eccetera et cetera
eccetto except
ecco here is, there is
economico inexpensive
l'edicola (f.) newsstand
l'edificio building
l'elenco list, directory
l'elettricità (f.) electricity
l'emergenza (f.) emergency
l'enoteca (f.) wine bar
entrambi both
entrare to enter
l'entrata (f.) entrance
l'Epifania (f.) Epiphany (Jan. 6)
esaurito sold out
esportare to export
espresso express
essenziale essential
essere (stato) to be
est east
l'estate (f.) summer
l'estero abroad
l'età (f.) age
l'etichetta (f.) tag, label
l'etto hectogram
l'Europa (f.) Europe
evitare to avoid

F

fa ago
la fabbrica (f.) factory
fabbricare to manufacture

la faccenda (f.)   thing, matter, chore
la faccia (f.)   face
facile   easy
la facoltà (f.)   school
il fagiolo   bean
la fame (f.)   hunger
la famiglia (f.)   family
famoso   famous
fare (fatto)   to do, to make
la farina (f.)   flour
la farmacia (f.)   pharmacy
la fatica (f.)   effort
il fatto   fact
la fattoria (f.)   farm
il fazzoletto   tissue
la febbre (f.)   fever
la fede (f.)   faith
felice   happy
la femmina (f.)   woman, female
la ferita (f.)   injury
la fermata (f.)   stop
Ferragosto   Assumption Day (Aug. 15)
la ferrovia (f.)   railroad
la festa (f.)   holiday
festeggiare   to celebrate
i fiammiferi (m. pl.)   matches
il fianco   side
la fidanzata (f.)   fiancée
il fidanzato   fiancé
fiero   proud
la fiera (f.)   fair
la figlia (f.)   daughter
il figlio   son
la fila (f.)   line, row
il filetto   filet
finalmente   finally
la finanza (f.)   finance
finanziare   to finance
la fine (f.)   end

il fine settimana   weekend
la finestra (f.)   window
fino a   until, as far as
la firma (f.)   signature
il fiume (m.)   river
il fuoco   fire
la foglia (f.)   leaf
il foglio   sheet of paper
il fondo   bottom
la fontana (f.)   fountain
le forbici (f. pl.)   scissors
la forchetta (f.)   fork
la foresta (f.)   forest
la forma (f.)   form
il formaggio   cheese
il fornaio   baker
il forno   oven
forse   maybe
forte   strong
la fortuna (f.)   fortune
la fotocopia (f.)   photocopy
la fotografia (f.)   photograph
fra   within, in, between, among
fragile   fragile
il francobollo   postage stamp
la frase (f.)   phrase, sentence
il fratello   brother
freddo   cold
fresco   fresh
la fretta (f.)   haste, hurry
fritto   fried
la frutta (f.)   fruit
il fruttivendolo   greengrocer's
fumare   to smoke
il funerale (m.)   funeral
la funivia (f.)   cable car, gondola
il fuoco   fire
fuori   outside
furbo   clever, sly (slang)

G

il gabinetto toilet
la galleria (f.) tunnel, gallery
la gamba (f.) leg
il gambero shrimp
il garage (m.) garage
garantire to guarantee
il gatto cat
il gelato ice-cream
il genero son-in-law
i genitori (m. pl.) parents
la gente (f.) people
gentile kind, polite
la gentilezza (f.) kindness
Gesù Jesus
il ghiaccio ice
già already
la giacca (f.) jacket
giallo yellow
il giardino garden
il ginecologo gynecologist
giocare to play
il giocattolo toy
il gioco game
la gioia (f.) joy
la gioielleria (f.) jewelry store
il giornalaio newspaper vendor
il giornale (m.) newspaper
la giornata (f.) day
il giorno day
giovane young
il giro tour
giù down
il giubbotto coat
la giurisprudenza (f.) law
giusto just, right, correct
la gonna (f.) skirt
il governo government
il grammo gram

grande big, large
la grappa (f.) grappa
grasso fat
gratis free of charge
grave serious, grave
la grazia (f.) grace
grazie! thank you!
la griglia (f.) grill
grosso large
la grotta (f.) cave
la gruccia (f.) hanger
i guanti (m. pl.) gloves
il guaio trouble
guardare to look at, to watch
il guardaroba (m.) cloakroom
guasto spoiled, rotten
il guasto breakdown
la guerra (f.) war
la guida (f.) guide
guidare to drive
gustare to taste
il gusto taste

H

la hostess (f.) stewardess
l'hotel (m.) hotel

I

I.V.A. (Imposta Valore Aggiunto) VAT/sales tax
l'identità (f.) identity
ieri yesterday
l'imbarco boarding
l'immagine (f.) image
l'immigrazione (f.) immigration
imparare to learn
l'impermeabile raincoat
l'impiegato worker,

employee, official
importante important
importare to import, to matter
l'impressione (f.) impression
in in, to, at
in fretta in a hurry
incartare to wrap
l'incidente (m.) accident
incinta pregnant
inciso engraved
incontrare to meet
l'incrocio crossing
l'indicazione (f.) direction, indication
indietro back, behind
l'indipendenza (f.) independence
indiretto indirect
l'indirizzo address
indossare to wear
infatti in fact
inferiore inferior, lower
l'infermiera (f.) nurse
l'inferno hell
l'informazione (f.) information
l'Inghilterra (f.) England
inglese English
ingrassare to gain weight
l'ingrediente (m.) ingredient
l'ingresso entrance
iniziare to begin
l'inizio beginning
innamorarsi to fall in love with
inoltre also
l'inquinamento pollution
l'insalata (f.) salad
l'insegnante (m./f.) teacher
insegnare to teach

l'insetto insect
insieme together
insolito unusual
interessante interesting
l'intermezzo intermission
interno internal, inside
interpretare to interpret
l'interprete interpreter
l'interurbana (f.) long-distance call
intorno a around
introdurre (introdotto) to introduce
inutile useless
invece instead
l'inverno winter
inviare to mail, to send
invitare to invite
l'invito invitation
io I
irregolare irregular
l'iscritto student, member
l'isola (f.) island
l'istruzione (f.) instruction
l'itinerario itinerary

J–K

i jeans (m. pl.) jeans

kasher kosher

L

là there
il ladro thief
il lago lake
la lampada (f.) light
la lampadina (f.) light bulb
il lampo lightning flash
il lampone (m.) raspberry
la lana (f.) wool

largo   wide
lasciare   to let, to leave behind
il lato   side
la latteria (f.)   dairy store
la lavanderia (f.)   laundry service
la lavanderia a secco   dry cleaner
il lavandino   sink
lavare   to wash
lavorare   to work
il lavoro   work
la legge (f.)   law
leggere (letto)   to read
leggero   light
il legno   wood
lei   she, her
Lei (polite)   you
il lenzuolo   sheet
la lettera (f.)   letter
il letto   bed
lì   there
libero   free
la libreria (f.)   bookstore
il libro   book
la linea (f.)   line
la lingua (f.)   language, tongue
la lista (f.)   list, menu
il litro   liter
lontano   far
loro   they
la lozione (f.)   lotion
la luce (f.)   light
lui   he, him
la luna (f.)   moon
la luna di miele (f.)   honeymoon
lunedì dell'Angelo   Easter Monday

la lunghezza (f.)   length
lungo   long
il luogo   place
lusso   luxury

M

ma   but
la macchia (f.)   stain
la macchina (f.)   automobile, car, machine
la macchina fotografica (f.)   camera
la macelleria (f.)   butcher shop
la madre (f.)   mother
la madrelingua (f.)   native language
il magazzino   department store
la maggioranza (f.)   majority
la maglia (f.)   sweater, pullover
magro   thin
mai   never, ever
il maiale (m.)   pork, pig
il mais (m.)   corn
malato   unhealthy, sick
la malattia (f.)   illness
la mancia (f.)   tip
mandare   to send
mangiare   to eat
la maniera (f.)   manner, way
la maniglia (f.)   handle
la mano (f.; pl. le mani)   hand
il manzo   beef
la marca (f.)   brand, type
il marciapiede (m.)   sidewalk
il mare (m.)   sea
la marea (f.)   tide

il **marito** husband
il **marmo** marble
marrone brown
la **mattina** (f.) morning
matto crazy
maturo ripe, mature
il **meccanico** mechanic
la **medicina** (f.) medicine
il **medico** doctor
il **Medioevo** Middle Ages
meglio better
meno less
la **mensa** (f.) cafeteria
mensile monthly
la **menta** (f.) mint
la **mente** (f.) mind
mentre while
il/la **mercante** (m./f.) merchant
il **mercato** market
la **merce** (f.) merchandise
il **mese** (m.) month
la **messa** (f.) mass
il **messaggio** message
la **metà** (f.) half
il **metallo** metal
la **metropolitana** (f.) subway
mettere (messo) to put, to place
la **mezzanotte** (f.) midnight
mezzo half
il **mezzo** means
mezzogiorno noon
mi me, to me
il **miele** (m.) honey
il **miglio** (pl. le miglia) mile
il/la **migliore** the best
la **minestra** (f.) soup
il **ministro** minister
la **minoranza** (f.) minority
minore smaller, less

il **minuto** minute
la **miseria** (f.) poverty
la **misura** (f.) measure, size
il/la **mittente** (m./f.) sender
il **mobile** (m.) piece of furniture
moderno modern
il **modo** manner, method, way
il **modulo** form
la **moglie** (f.) wife
molto a lot, much, very
il **momento** moment
il **mondo** world
la **moneta** (f.) coin
monolocale (m.) single room, studio
la **montagna** (f.) mountain
il **monumento** monument
morbido soft, smooth
morire (morto) to die
la **morte** (f.) death
la **mosca** (f.) fly (insect)
la **mostra** (f.) show (art)
il **motore** (m.) motor
il **motorino** scooter
la **multa** (f.) fine, ticket
il **muro** wall
il **museo** museum
mussulmano Muslim
il **mutuo** loan

N

la **nascita** (f.) birth
il **nastro** tape
la **natura** (f.) nature
naturale natural
la **nave** (f.) ship
la **nazionalità** (f.) nationality
la **nazione** (f.) nation

ne some of, about it
né ... né neither ... nor
neanche not even
la nebbia (f.) fog
la necessità (f.) need, necessity
necessario necessary
il negozio shop
nemmeno not even
nessuno no one, nobody
la neve (f.) snow
niente nothing
il nipote grandson, nephew
la nipote (f.) granddaughter, niece
la nocciola (f.) hazelnut
la nocciolina (f.) peanut
la noce (f.) walnut
noi we
noioso boring
noleggiare to rent
il nome (m.) noun, name
il nome da nubile maiden name
il nome del coniuge name of spouse
il nome di famiglia surname
non not
la nonna (f.) grandmother
il nonno grandfather
nord north
la notizia (f.) news
la notte (f.) night
la novità (f.) news
nubile unmarried
nulla nothing
il numero number
il numero verde toll-free number
la nuora (f.) daughter-in-law
nuotare to swim
nuovo new

O

o or
l'occasione (f.) occasion, bargain
gli occhiali (m. pl.) eyeglasses
l'occhio eye
l'Occidente West
occupato busy, occupied
l'oceano ocean
l'odore (m.) aroma, odor
l'offerta (f.) offer
gli oggetti smarriti (m. pl.) lost property
l'oggetto object
oggi today
ogni each, every
Ognissanti All Saint's Day (Nov. 1)
ognuno everybody
l'olio oil
l'oliva (f.) olive
oltre more than, in addition to
l'ombrello umbrella
l'onda (f.) wave
onesto honest
l'operaio worker
oppure or
l'ora (f.) hour, now
l'ora di punta (f.) rush hour
l'orario schedule
l'ordine (m.) order
l'oreficeria (f.) jeweler's, goldsmith's
orgoglioso proud
Oriente East, Orient
l'oro gold
l'orologio watch, clock
l'orto garden
l'ospedale (m.) hospital

l'ospite (m./f.) guest
l'ostello hostel
ottico optician
ottimo excellent, best
l'ottone brass
ovest west
ovunque wherever

P

il pacco package, parcel
la pace (f.) peace
il padre (m.) father
il padrino godfather
il padrone/la padrona (f.)
boss, landlord, owner
il paese (m.) country, town
pagare to pay
il palazzo building, palace
il palco box (theater)
il palcoscenico stage
la palestra (f.) gym
la palla (f.) ball
la pallacanestro (f.) basketball
la palude (f.) swamp, marsh
il pane (m.) bread
la panetteria (f.) bakery
il panino sandwich
la panna (f.) cream
il pannolino diaper
il panorama (m.) panorama,
view
i pantaloni (m. pl.) pants
il Papa (m.) Pope
il papà (m.) daddy, pop
il parcheggio parking lot
il parco park
il/la parente (m./f.) relative
parere (parso) to seem, to
appear
la partenza (f.) departure

partire to depart, to leave
la partita (f.) game, match
Pasqua Easter
il passaporto passport
passare to pass
il passato past
la passeggiata (f.) stroll, walk
la passione (f.) passion
il passo step
la pasticceria (f.) pastry shop
il pasto meal
la patente (f.) driver's license
la patria (f.) homeland
il patrigno stepfather
la paura (f.) fear
il pavimento floor
peccato! what a shame!
il pedaggio toll
il pelo hair
la pelle (f.) skin, leather
la pelletteria (f.) furrier
shop
la pelliccia (f.) fur
la pellicola (f.) film
la pena (f.) penalty
la penisola (f.) peninsula
la penna (f.) pen
pensare to think
la pensione (f.) inn, pension
il pepe (m.) pepper
per for, in order to
per favore please
per piacere please
il percento percentage
perché why, because
il percorso route
perdere (perso) to lose
il pericolo danger
pericoloso dangerous
la periferia (f.) suburbs
permesso! excuse me!

permettere (permesso) to permit

però but, however

la persona (f.) person

pesante heavy

il pesce (m.) fish

la pescheria (f.) fish store

il peso weight

il piacere (m.) pleasure

piacevole pleasing

piangere (pianto) to cry

il pianterreno ground floor

il piano floor, (adv.) softly

la pianta (f.) plant

la pianura (f.) plain

il piatto plate

la piazza (f.) town square

piccante spicy

il picco peak

piccolo small

il piede (m.) foot

pieno full

la pietra (f.) stone

la pila (f.) battery

la pillola (f.) pill

la pioggia (f.) rain

piovere to rain

la piscina (f.) swimming pool

la pista (f.) track, trail, slope

la pittura (f.) painting

più more

piuttosto rather

il pneumatico tire

un po' a little

poco not very much

poi then, afterward

poiché since

la politica (f.) politics

la polizia (f.) police

il poliziotto police officer

la polpetta (f.) meatball

il pomeriggio afternoon

il pomodoro tomato

il pompiere (m.) firefighter

il ponte (m.) bridge

il porco pig, pork

la porta (f.) door

il portabagagli (m.) porter

il portacenere (m.) ashtray

il portafoglio wallet

portare to bring, to carry

il porto harbor, port

la porzione (f.) portion

la posta (f.) mail, post office

il postino postal carrier

il posto seat, place

potere to be able to

pranzare to dine, to eat lunch

il pranzo lunch, supper

pratico convenient, practical

il prato field

il prefisso area code

pregare to pray, to beg, to ask

la preghiera (f.) prayer

prego! you are welcome!

prendere (preso) to take

prenotare to make a reservation

la prenotazione (f.) reservation

preoccupato worried

presentare to present

il presente (m.) present

presso in care of (c/o)

prestare to lend

presto quickly, early

il prete (m.) priest

il prezzo price

il prezzo d'entrata admission charge

prima before

la primavera (f.) spring

primo first, before
il problema (m.) problem
il profilattico condom
la profumeria (f.) cosmetics shop
il profumo perfume
il programma (m.) plan, program
promettere (promesso) to promise
pronto ready, hello (telephone)
pronto soccorso first aid
la pronuncia (f.) pronunciation
pronunciare to pronounce
il proprietario owner
la proprietà privata (f.) private property
proprio just, really
prossimo next
provare to try, to experience
il pubblico public
pulire to clean
il pullman (m.) bus
purché provided that
pure also

Q

qua here
il quadro painting, picture
qualche some
qualche volta sometimes
qualcosa something
qualcuno someone
quale which
qualsiasi any
qualunque any
quando when
quanto? how much?

il quartiere (m.) neighborhood
quasi almost
quattordici fourteen
quello/quella that
la questione (f.) matter
questo this one
la questura (f.) police headquarters
qui here
quindi therefore
quotidiano daily (adj.)
il quotidiano daily paper

R

il rabbino rabbi
il raffreddore (m.) cold
la ragazza (f.) girl
il ragazzo boy
rallentare slow down
il rapido express train
la rapina (f.) robbery
il rapporto relationship
recente recent
il regalo gift, present
la regione (f.) region
il/la regista (m./f.) movie director
la religione (f.) religion
la residenza (f.) residence
restare to remain, to stay
il resto remainder, rest
ricco rich
la ricetta (f.) recipe, prescription
il ricevimento reception
la ricevuta (f.) receipt
la richiesta (f.) request
ricordare to remember
ridere (riso) to laugh

riempire to fill out (a form)
i rifiuti (m. pl.) trash
riflettere (riflesso) to reflect
il rifugio refuge
rilassante relaxing
rimanere (rimasto) to remain
il rimborso refund
il Rinascimento the Renaissance
ringraziare to thank
riparare to repair
ripetere to repeat
riscaldare to warm, to heat
la riserva d'acqua (f.) reservoir
la riserva naturale (f.) nature preserve
riservato reserved
la risposta (f.) answer, response
il ristorante (m.) restaurant
il ritardo delay
il ritmo rhythm
ritornare to return
il ritratto portrait
la rivista (f.) magazine
la roba (f.) stuff, things
la roccia (f.) rock
il romanzo novel, fiction, romance
rotto broken
le rovine (f. pl.) ruins
rubare to steal
il rubinetto faucet
rumoroso noisy
la rupe (f.) cliff
il ruscello stream

S

la sabbia (f.) sand
il sacco a pelo sleeping bag

la sala (f.) room, hall
la sala d'attesa (f.) waiting room
la sala da pranzo (f.) dining room
la sala giochi (f.) game room
il saldo sale, discount
il sale (m.) salt
salire to climb, to mount
il salotto living room, lounge
la salsa (f.) sauce
la salute (f.) health
il sangue (m.) blood
il santo/la santa (f.) saint
il sapone (m.) soap
il sapore (m.) taste
il sarto tailor
sbagliare to be mistaken
sbarcare to land, to disembark
la scala (f.) stairs
scambiare to exchange
lo scambio exchange
lo scapolo bachelor
la scarpa (f.) shoe
la scatola (f.) box
scegliere (scelto) to choose
scemo silly, idiotic
la scena (f.) scene
scendere to descend, to get off
scherzare to joke
lo schizzo sketch
lo sci (m.) skiing
lo sci di fondo cross-country skiing
la sciarpa (f.) scarf
scomodo uncomfortable
lo sconto discount
lo scontrino receipt
la scrivania (f.) desk
scrivere (scritto) to write

la **scultura** (f.) sculpture
la **scuola** (f.) school
scuro dark
scusarsi to apologize
se if
sé oneself (himself, herself …)
sebbene although
secco dry
sedersi to sit down
la **sedia** (f.) chair
il **segnale** (m.) signal, sign
segnare to mark, to note
il **segno** sign
seguente following
seguire to follow
la **selva** (f.) woods, forest
il **semaforo** traffic light
sembrare to seem
semplice simple
sempre always
senso unico one-way street
il **sentiero** path, track
il **sentimento** feeling, sentiment
sentire to hear, to smell, to taste
senza without
la **sera** (f.) evening
il **serbatoio** gas tank
sereno calm, good weather
serio serious
il **servizio** service
il **sesso** sex
la **sete** (f.) thirst
la **settimana** (f.) week
si oneself, each other, one, they
sì yes
la **signora** (f.) Mrs., Ms., woman

il **signore** (m.) Mr., Sir, man
la **signorina** (f.) Miss, young lady
simpatico nice, kind
la **sinfonia** (f.) symphony
singolo single
sinistro left
il **sintomo** symptom
smettere (smesso) to quit
la **società** (f.) company
soffice soft
solamente only
i **soldi** (m. pl.) money
il **sole** (m.) sun
solito usual
solo alone
il **sonno** sleep
sono I am, they are
sopra above, on
la **sorella** (f.) sister
la **sorellastra** (f.) stepsister, half-sister
la **sorgente** (f.) spring
la **sosta** (f.) stop, pause
sotto beneath
il **sottotitolo** subtitle
spaventare to scare, to frighten
la **spazzatura** (f.) trash can
la **spazzola** (f.) brush
lo **spazzolino da denti** toothbrush
lo **specchio** mirror
la **specie** (f.) type, kind
spedire to send
la **spesa** (f.) expense, shopping
spesso often
lo **spettacolo** show
la **spiaggia** (f.) beach
sporco dirty

lo sportello   counter, window

sposare   to marry

sposato   married

lo spumante (m.)   sparkling wine

lo spuntino   snack

lo stadio   stadium

la stagione (f.)   season

stamattina   this morning

stanco   tired

stanotte   tonight

la stanza (f.)   room

stare (stato)   to be, to remain, to stay

stasera   this evening

gli Stati Uniti (m. pl.) United States

la stazione (f.)   station

stesso   same

lo stivale (m.)   boot

la stoffa (f.)   fabric, cloth

la strada (f.)   street

lo straniero   foreigner, (adj.) foreign

stretto   tight

su, sul, sulla   on top of, on, up

subito   soon, immediately

succedere (successo)   to happen

il succo   juice

sud   south

la suocera (f.)   mother-in-law

il suocero   father-in-law

il supermercato   supermarket

la sveglia (f.)   alarm clock

la svendita (f.)   sale

T

la tabaccheria (f.)   tobacco shop

la tabella (f.)   schedule, time table

la taglia (f.)   size

tale   such, like, similar

tanto   so much, so many, a lot

tardi   late

la tariffa (f.)   fare, charge

la tassa (f.)   tax

il tassì (m.)   taxi

la tavola (f.)   dinner table

il tavolo   table (restaurant)

la tazza (f.)   cup

te   you (familiar)

il tè (m.)   tea

il teatro   theater

telefonare   to telephone

la telefonata (f.)   telephone call

il tempo   weather, time

tenere   to hold, to keep

la terra (f.)   earth, dirt

il terrazzo   terrace

la tessera (f.)   card, ticket

la testa (f.)   head

il tetto   roof

il tipo   type, kind

tirare   to pull

toccare   to touch

la toilette (f.)   toilet

il topo   mouse

tornare   to return

la torta (f.)   cake

il torto   wrong, fault

il tovagliolo   napkin

tra   between

tradurre (tradotto)   to translate

la **traduzione** (f.)   translation
il **traffico**   traffic
il **traghetto**   ferry
il **tramonto**   sunset
il **treno**   train
triste   sad
trovare   to find
tu   you (familiar)
il **tuono**   thunder
il **turismo**   tourism
il/la **turista** (m./f.)   tourist
tutt'e due   both
tuttavia   however, yet
tutti   everyone
tutto   everything, all

U

ubriacarsi   to get drunk
l'**uccello**   bird
l'**ufficio cambio**   money exchange office
l'**ufficio informazioni** information office
l'**ufficio oggetti smarriti** lost and found
l'**ufficio postale**   post office
ultimo   last
l'**umidità** (f.)   humidity
un   a, an, one
una   a, an, one
uno   one, a, an
l'**uomo**   man
l'**uovo** (pl. le uova)   egg
usare   to use
uscire   to exit
l'**uscita** (f.)   exit
l'**uva** (f.)   grapes

V

la **vacanza** (f.)   vacation
il **vaglia postale** (m.)   money order
il **vagone** (m.)   rail car
la **valigia** (f.)   bag, valise, suitcase
la **valuta** (f.)   currency, money
la **vasca** (f.)   tub
vecchio   old
vedere (visto)   to see
il **veicolo**   vehicle
vegetariano   vegetarian
il **veleno**   poison
vendere   to sell
la **vendità** (f.)   sale
venire   to come
veramente   really
verde   green
la **verdura** (f.)   vegetables
la **verità** (f.)   truth
verso   toward, near, about
il **vescovo**   bishop
vestire   to dress
il **vestito**   dress, suit
la **vetrina** (f.)   shop window
il **vetro**   glass
la **vettura** (f.)   carriage, railroad car
la **via** (f.)   street, way
via   away
viaggiare   to travel
il **viaggio**   trip
il **viale** (m.)   boulevard, avenue
vicino   near (adj.)
il **vicolo**   alley, lane
vietato   prohibited
vietato di sosta   no parking

vietato l'ingresso no entrance
il vigile police officer
il vigile del fuoco fire-fighter
vincere (vinto) to win
il vino wine
la vista (f.) view
la vita (f.) life
il vitello veal
il vocabolario vocabulary
la voce (f.) voice
la voglia (f.) wish, desire
voi you (plural)
volare to fly
volentieri! gladly!
volere to want
il volo flight
vuoto empty

Y

lo yoga (m.) yoga
lo yogurt (m.) yogurt

Z

lo zaino backpack
la zanzara (f.) mosquito
la zia (f.) aunt
lo zio uncle
lo zucchero sugar
la zuppa (f.) soup

Index

Frame "Mille flori"
mosaic glass